From Shanghai to the Burma Railway

From Shanghai to the Burma Railway

The Memoirs & Letters of Richard Laird

A Japanese Prisoner of War

Edited by

Rory Laird

Pen & Sword
MILITARY
AN IMPRINT OF PEN & SWORD BOOKS LTD.
YORKSHIRE – PHILADELPHIA

First published in Great Britain in 2020 by
Pen & Sword Military
An imprint of
Pen & Sword Books Ltd
Yorkshire – Philadelphia

Copyright © Rory Laird 2020

ISBN 978 1 52677 111 7

The right of Rory Laird to be identified as Author of this work has been asserted by him in accordance with the Copyright, Designs and Patents Act 1988.

A CIP catalogue record for this book is
available from the British Library.

All rights reserved. No part of this book may be reproduced or transmitted in any form or by any means, electronic or mechanical including photocopying, recording or by any information storage and retrieval system, without permission from the Publisher in writing.

Printed and bound in the UK by TJ International Ltd, Padstow, Cornwall.

Pen & Sword Books Limited incorporates the imprints of Atlas, Archaeology, Aviation, Discovery, Family History, Fiction, History, Maritime, Military, Military Classics, Politics, Select, Transport, True Crime, Air World, Frontline Publishing, Leo Cooper, Remember When, Seaforth Publishing, The Praetorian Press, Wharncliffe Local History, Wharncliffe Transport, Wharncliffe True Crime and White Owl.

For a complete list of Pen & Sword titles please contact

PEN & SWORD BOOKS LIMITED
47 Church Street, Barnsley, South Yorkshire, S70 2AS, England
E-mail: enquiries@pen-and-sword.co.uk
Website: www.pen-and-sword.co.uk

Or
PEN AND SWORD BOOKS
1950 Lawrence Rd, Havertown, PA 19083, USA
E-mail: Uspen-and-sword@casematepublishers.com
Website: www.penandswordbooks.com

*In grateful thanks to my parents,
Dickie and Bobbie,
and
for Richard, Alex and Will
and their families,
that they may remember.*

Contents

Introduction		xi
Sources and Acknowledgement		xv
List of Maps		xvii
Chapter 1	Shanghai 1937 to 1939	1
Chapter 2	Singapore and Penang 1939 to 1941	35
Chapter 3	Prisoner of War – Changi February 1942 to April 1943	69
Chapter 4	Prisoner of War – 'F' Force and the Burma Railway April to December 1943	81
Chapter 5	Prisoner of War – Changi and Freedom December 1943 to October 1945	109
Postscript		141
Appendix I	Narrative of 'F' Force in Thailand April to December 1943 Captain (later Lieutenant Colonel) Cyril H.D. Wild (Ox & Bucks LI)	145
Appendix II	Report on Prisoners of War in Thailand May to December 1943 Lieutenant Colonel F.J. Dillon, OBE, MC (AA & QMG 18 Div)	153
Appendix III	Tanbaya Hospital Burma – Medical Report 1 August to 24 November 1943 Major Bruce Hunt, AAMC, Commanding Burma Hospital	165
Bibliography and Suggested Further Reading		173
Index		175

List of Maps

Shanghai – The International Settlement 1935	xvii
Malaya – The Japanese Advance, December 1941 to February 1942	xviii
Dutch East Indies 1942 – Bobbie's Escape Route to Batavia and Australia	xix
Singapore Island 1942	xx
The Burma Siam Railway and Work Camps 1943	xxi

Introduction

My father, Richard ('Dick' or 'Dickie') Laird, was born in Birkenhead in 1911. His father, Roy MacGregor Laird ('RML') was a member of the Cammell Laird shipbuilding dynasty, who had married his cousin Mary in 1901. Richard was the fourth of six children, and was to become particularly close to his elder brother, Henry, and his immediate elder sister Marjorie, or 'Maudie' as she was known. The family lived comfortably in Birkenhead, but were devastated by Mary's death in the Spanish influenza epidemic in 1919. RML subsequently married her younger sister, Winifred, who had been widowed at the young age of 31. When RML retired in 1928, he moved the family to High Lindeth, Bowness-on-Windermere in the Lake District, but sadly was not to enjoy his retirement, dying later that same year.

Fairly soon after this, the family started to fragment. In 1929 Maudie married a naval officer, Colin Gatey (whose father Norman Gatey was a solicitor in the firm Gatey Heelis, and was a partner of Beatrix Potter's husband William Heelis). Later the same year Henry married Barbara ('Barbie') Faraday and moved to Derby to join a small engineering company, Michael McEvoy, which specialised in high-speed development of motor cars. Winifred, now twice widowed before her fortieth birthday, sold the High Lindeth house in 1930 and moved south taking the two youngest sisters with her.

Richard, after school at Harrow, departed to Cambridge University, splitting his vacations between Henry and Barbie in Duffield, Derbyshire, and walking holidays in the Bavarian Alps. There he lodged with the family of the late Friedrich von Duhn, former Professor of Archaeology at Heidelberg University. His experiences there of the growing influence of Adolf Hitler and the Nazi Party coloured his views considerably, and led him to join the Territorial Army, although he nevertheless remained a strong advocate of appeasement providing it was backed by a realistic programme of preparation for war.

Henry was by now McEvoy's leading demonstrator of go-faster motoring equipment, and had started to invest his inheritance in Morgan three-wheelers, owning six in all, but finally settling on two. One, known as 'Yellow', was a trials car that Henry, with Barbie in the passenger seat, drove on long-distance trials all over the UK and Europe, competing against motor cycles and side car combinations with great success. The other, known as 'Red', was an out-and-out race car enhanced by a Zoller supercharger in which Henry, with his brother Richard in the passenger seat (the Auto-Cycle Union would not then allow ladies in race cars), raced at Brooklands, Donnington and elsewhere. In the meantime, Richard had spent his inheritance on a succession of Brough Superior motorbikes (then the 'Rolls Royce' of motor cycles), which he also rode on long-distance trials throughout the UK. These activities kept the Laird brothers well occupied for five years from 1932 to 1937, and probably accounted for Richard's third class history degree from Trinity College, Cambridge.

In 1937, having gone to work in London for the Sun Insurance Office Limited, Richard was offered a posting to their office in Shanghai. Disillusioned with life in London, and conscious of the rising threat of another European war, he accepted with alacrity. After two years in Shanghai, including service with the Shanghai Volunteer Corps during the 1937 Sino-Japanese Hostilities, in 1939 he was moved to the Sun office in Singapore.

It was there, as Best Man at a friend's wedding in June 1940, that he met the Chief Bridesmaid, Erika ('Bobbie') Couper Patrick, the girl who was ultimately to become his wife. Bobbie was a

Shanghai girl. Her Scottish father, Harry Couper Patrick, was a doctor who, having worked for a number of years in India, then moved to Sydney, where he married an Australian, Ida Garvin, the daughter of the Inspector General of the New South Wales Police. Shortly afterwards they moved to Shanghai, where Bobbie was born in 1911, and lived there until 1941. In December 1941 Bobbie moved to Singapore to work for the Oriental Mission of the Special Operations Executive (SOE) as a secretary. There she renewed her acquaintance with Richard, and they became 'unofficially engaged' on Christmas Eve 1941, seven weeks before the fall of Singapore to the invading Japanese army, and in the full knowledge of the uncertainties to come. Bobbie escaped from Singapore at the beginning of February 1942 to continue her work with SOE in Batavia, Melbourne (Australia) and Colombo (Ceylon) until 1945. Richard was not so fortunate, and became a prisoner-of-war, initially in Changi, and later on the Burma–Siam Railway. He was ultimately reunited with Bobbie in Colombo in October 1945.

This book tells the full story in their own words, through Richard's memoir and extracts from their letters.

The Memoir and Letters. My father wrote his memoir in 1987, some forty to fifty years after the events it describes, giving it the title *The Best Years of My Life* – on the face of it a strange title for a memoir covering a period of considerable excitement, but also immense uncertainty and almost unimaginable suffering. As he himself makes clear in the opening paragraph, he chose that title because it was a time when he was more conscious of being alive than at any time previously or subsequently. He wrote the original in longhand, illustrated with photographs (mostly his own). He then had the original and three copies bound in hard covers for the benefit of his family. Over the years covered by the memoir, he also wrote a number of letters to his elder sister Maudie in England, and later to my mother, Bobbie. She also wrote quite a number of letters to him, only the later ones of which I still have. Sadly, none of the 27 or more 25-word Red Cross letters she sent him while he was a prisoner of war have survived, although a number of the accompanying photographs have. I have included extracts from a number of the surviving letters chronologically within the memoir to give it a more immediate feel; the memoir is 'history', the letters are 'contemporary'. I have not altered the letters; the language they use and the views and perceptions they express are of their time; they may not be 'politically correct' but they are a true record of the world as seen through the eyes of two young people living through a time of great turbulence and uncertainty.

To differentiate between the two, the memoir is written in a plain text font, and the letters and a diary transcript are written in an indented smaller text font. At the start of each chapter and the appendices there is *an editorial section in italics* to explain the historical context, and elaborate on some of the personalities mentioned. Within the body of the text of each chapter there are also brief editorial notes [*italicized in square brackets*] to explain acronyms, or to elaborate slightly on the original text. Place names are those that were in use at the time.

This is a story of remarkable fortitude and belief; without being overly romantic, it is also a story that demonstrates the power of friendship and love to see people through the darkest of times. Although the memoir and letters were not written for publication, now, 25 years after Bobbie's death and more than 10 years after Richard's death, seems an appropriate time for their story, remarkable even by the standards of that understated but extraordinary wartime generation, to reach a wider audience. I hope you enjoy reading it, as much as I have enjoyed putting it together.

Rory Laird
Dollar, 2019

Sources and Acknowledgement

First and foremost, I have to thank my parents, Richard (Dickie) and Bobbie, not only for their prolific letter and memoir writing, but for keeping their pre-war and wartime letters so that now, eighty years on, their extraordinary wartime experiences can be brought to life for a wider audience. Richard's collection of photographs that he took himself in Shanghai and pre-war Singapore also help to illuminate the memoir and letters in a fascinating way. Since none of his wartime photographs survived captivity, the photographs illustrating the sections covering his time as a prisoner of war of the Japanese are from the collections of the Australian War Memorial. Those of Selarang Barracks and the 'F' Force Songkurai work camps were taken by an Australian prisoner, Private George Aspinall, who, at great risk to himself, smuggled his folding Six-20 Kodak Brownie camera into captivity. While they are not of the highest quality, it is not surprising considering the conditions under which they were taken, and the fact that the negatives had to be buried in containers at Changi to avoid discovery by the Japanese; it is a wonder that they survived at all. My thanks also to George Connor, Sherwood and Betty Connor's son, for agreeing to my use of the photograph of his parents on page 9 of the plate section. Richard's large collection of books about the war in the Far East have also been invaluable in helping me to elaborate a little on the historical context of his memoir and letters, and on some of the remarkable characters that crossed his path in Singapore and on the Burma Railway. I must also thank Hamish Brown, noted Scottish mountaineer and prolific author, for the inspiration to publish my father's memoir and letters that came from his book *East of West, West of East* which describes his own family's wartime experiences in Malaya and Singapore. His subsequent encouragement and assistance has been invaluable. My own family, Shelagh my wife, and our sons Richard, Alex and Will, have also played their part in patiently supporting my endeavours, and in proofreading and commenting on my text. Finally I must thank the team at Pen and Sword for all the help and advice they have provided to a complete newcomer to the world of publishing. In particular I would thank Henry Wilson for allowing himself to be persuaded to take it on in the first place; Matt Jones and all of the production team for bringing the project to fruition; Barnaby Blacker, my copy editor, for his wise counsel; and Jon Wilkinson for his work on the jacket design.

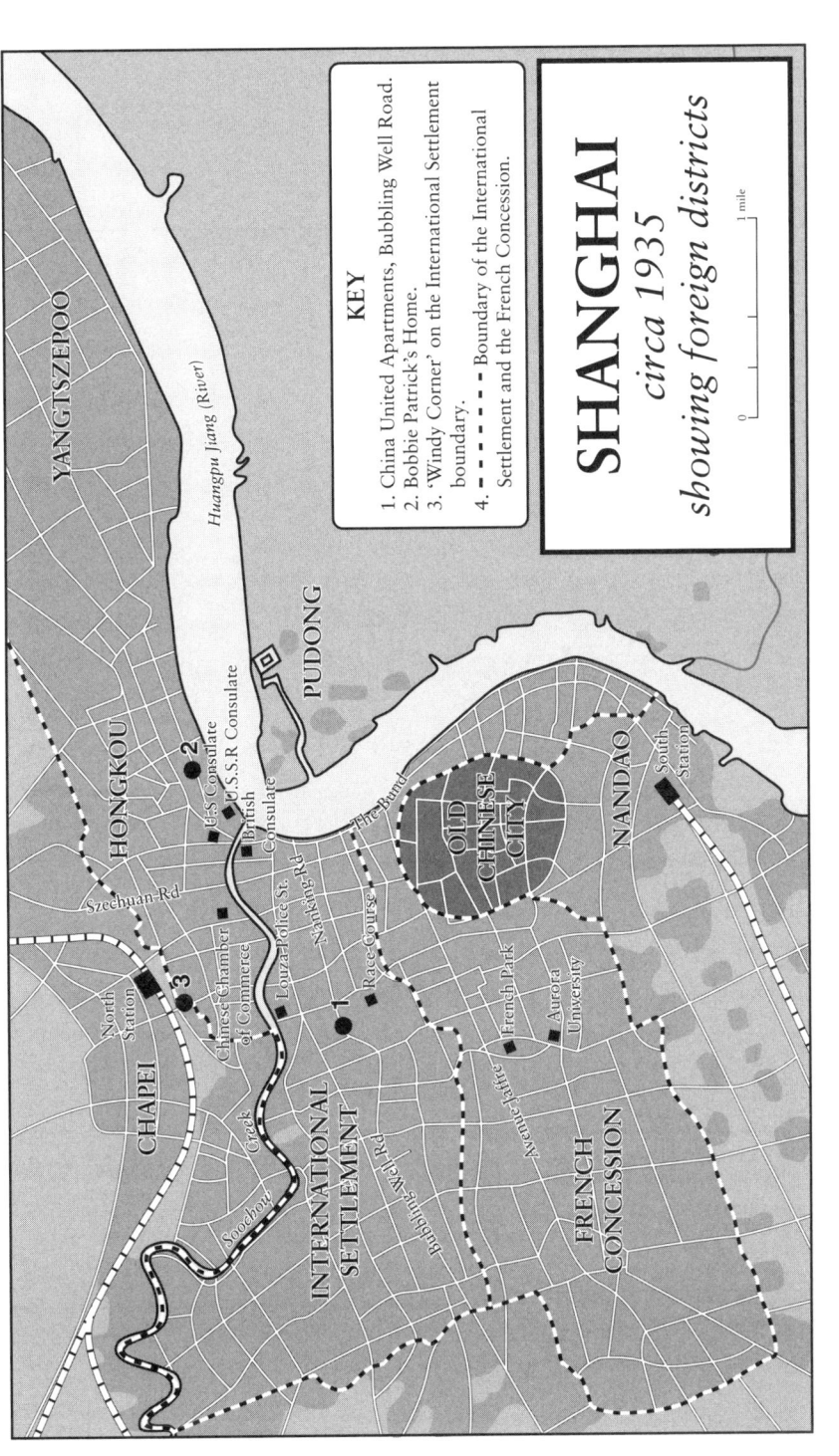

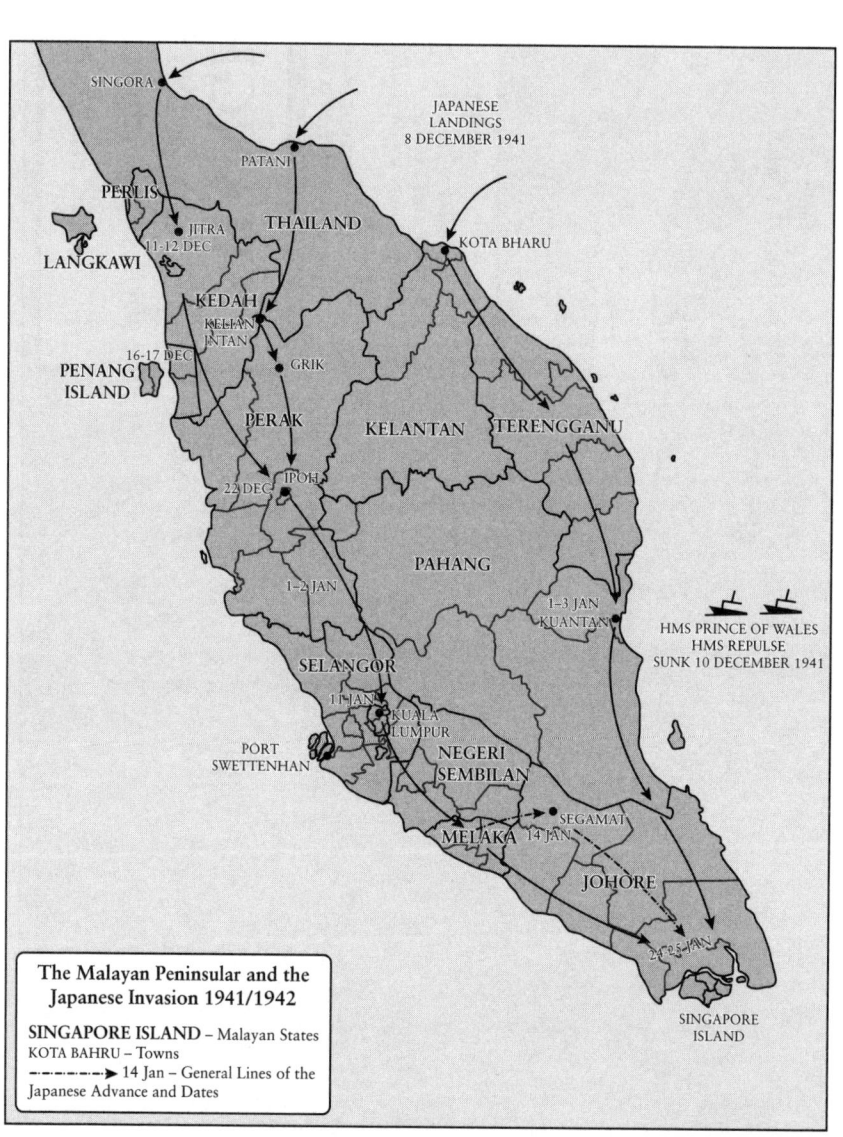

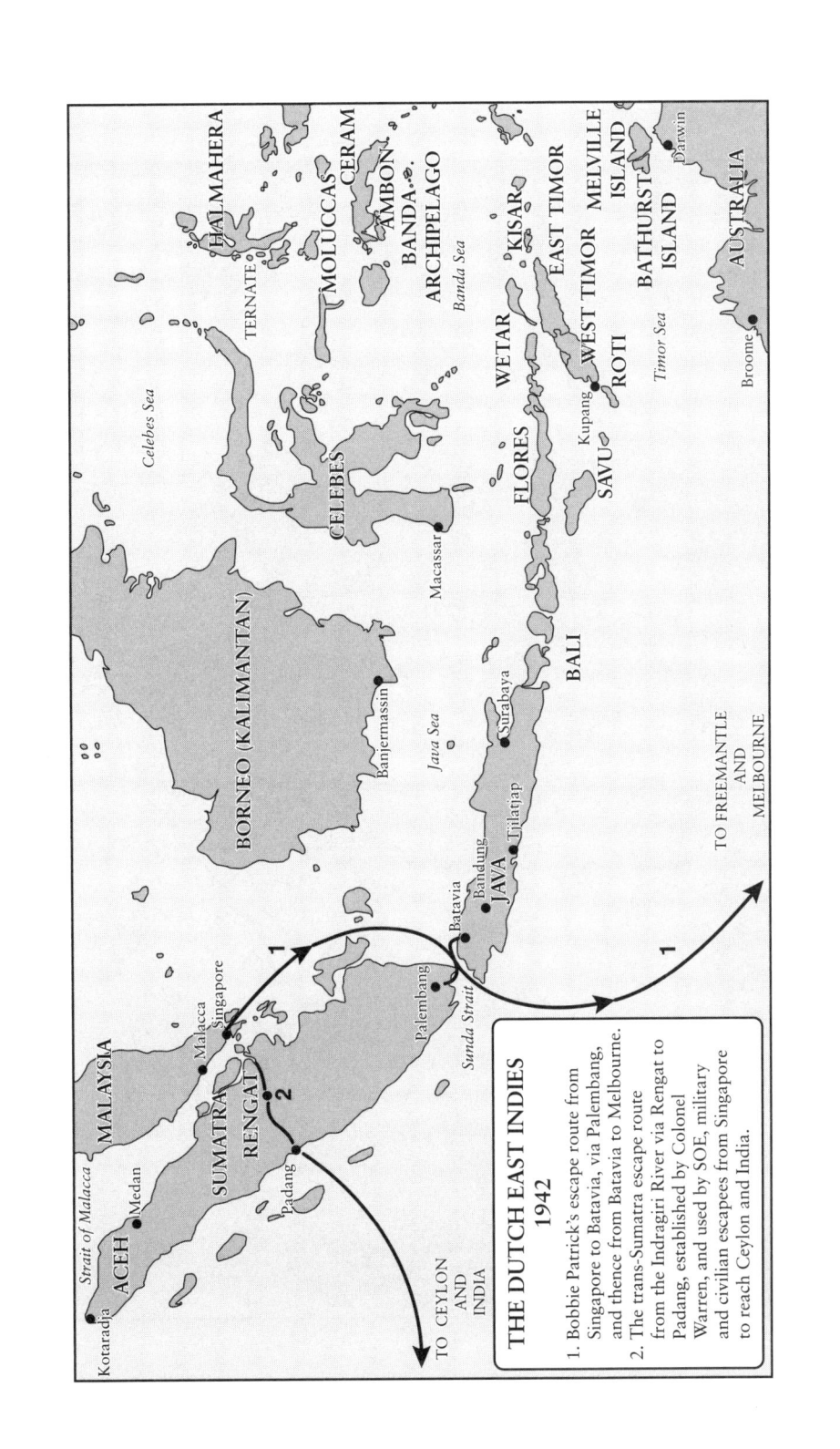

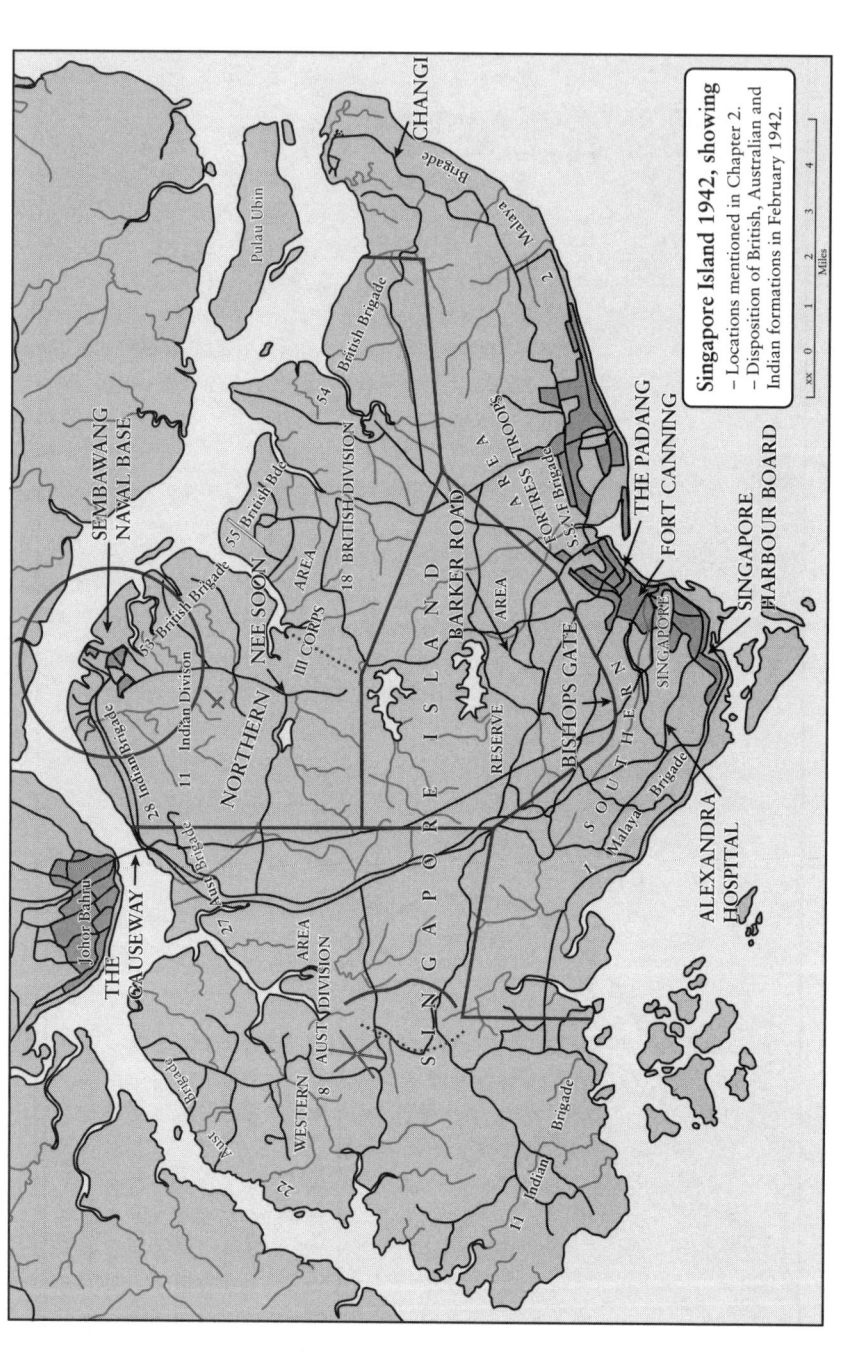

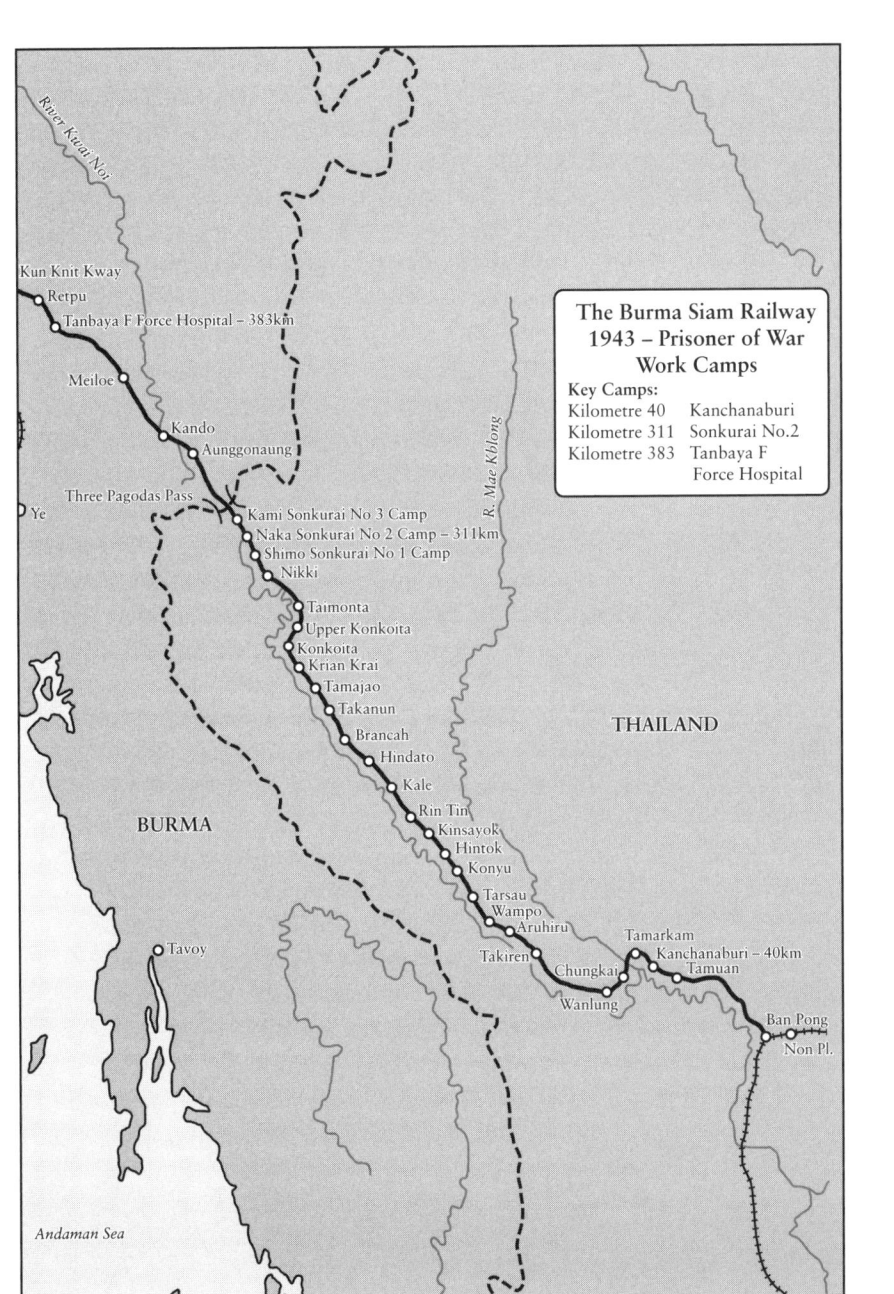

Chapter One

Shanghai 1937 to 1939

Shanghai was one of the first group of five treaty ports set up under the Treaty of Nanking in 1842 following China's defeat by Britain in the First Opium War, to allow western powers access to China for trade. Ultimately over eighty such treaty ports were established during the nineteenth century by a series of treaties (the 'unequal treaties') by the Qing dynasty after military attacks or threats by foreign powers. The system lasted for a hundred years, between 1841 and 1941. In the first half of the twentieth century Shanghai was a thriving and very cosmopolitan city, and one of the largest in the world with a population in 1936 of around 3 million. Of these about 50,000 were of European origin, including some 35,000 Russian refugees from the Revolution. There was also a substantial, and growing, Japanese population. The Europeans lived and worked predominantly in the International Settlement and the French Concession.

The International Settlement and the French Concession. The Shanghai International Settlement originated from the 1863 merger of the British and American enclaves in Shanghai, the French having made a separate agreement with the Chinese in 1854, their territory being known as the French Concession. These settlements had initially been established in 1843 under the Treaty of Nanking, when territorial concessions were granted to the British, Americans and French. These concessions remained in Chinese ownership and were only leased to the respective governments. It was within the International Settlement that Richard, in common with nearly all other Europeans, lived *and worked. From around 1915, the Japanese became the most numerous foreign power resident in the International Settlement, mostly settling in the area of Hongkew (Hongkou). Following the second Sino-Japanese War in 1937, the Japanese military took over the whole of Shanghai outside the boundaries of the International Settlement and the French Concession. In December 1941, following the attack on the American Naval Base at Pearl Harbor, the Japanese occupied the International Settlement and interned all foreign nationals living within it. The survivors were released in August 1945, at which time the International Settlement reverted to Chinese control, the French Concession following suit in 1946.*

<u>*The China United Apartments.*</u> *When he first arrived in Shanghai in April 1937, Richard lived in an apartment block within the International Settlement close to the Race Course, named the China United Apartments. Although he was not to meet her until three years later in Singapore, my mother Bobbie also lived in the China United Apartments. The building, dating from 1929 and built by the China United Assurance Company, still stands, and is now a Chinese-owned hotel, the Pacific Hotel. My wife Shelagh and I stayed there during a visit to Shanghai in 2011; it was a strange feeling being in the building where both my parents had lived seventy-four years previously. The Race Course on which Richard played cricket and tennis is now the Peoples' Square, largely concreted over but with some attractive ornamental gardens, and a very large metro station underneath it. The original 1933 art deco Shanghai Race Club building also still stands, and now houses the Shanghai Art Museum. Bobbie worked in an office in the same building as the Cathay Hotel on the corner of Nanking Road and The Bund (No.20 The Bund). It was built between 1926 and 1929 by Victor Sassoon and, like all the grand early twentieth century buildings on The Bund overlooking the Whampoa (Huangpu) River, it still stands; it was renamed the Peace Hotel in 1956. Richard's office was also*

on The Bund, in No.1 The Bund, then known as the McBain Building, housing, amongst others, the offices of Royal Dutch Shell and the Asiatic Petroleum Company. It is now known as The Asia Building.

<u>*The Shanghai Sino-Japanese Hostilities 1937*</u>*. The orderly life, both commercial and social, of the International Settlement in Shanghai, was to be seriously, and irrevocably, disrupted in August 1937 when the Sino-Japanese Hostilities broke out. These occurred during the initial stages of the Second Sino-Japanese War, which was the result of decades-long Japanese imperialist policy. In 1931 the Japanese had invaded Manchuria, and from 1931 to 1937 China and Japan continued to skirmish in small, localised engagements. In July 1937 however, Japan attacked and captured Peking [Beijing]. In response the Chinese commander, Chiang Kai-shek, laid siege to the Japanese area of the International Settlement in Shanghai. Having failed to evict the Japanese in the early stages of this engagement, the Chinese forces were ultimately defeated by the heavily reinforced Japanese army which captured Shanghai (with the exception of the International Settlement and the French Concession) in November 1937.*

Turning now to Richard's memoir and letters...

It may seem strange to describe the period 1936 to 1945 as 'the best years of my life' considering that they cover World War II (and, in my case, three and a half years as a prisoner of war of the Japanese) but these were the years when I was more conscious of being alive than at any time before or since: also it was a time when I met – and fell for the girl who was to become such an important part of my life, and, after quite a saga for both of us, my wife – Bobbie Patrick.

I have taken 1936 as the starting point of this memoir because in August of that year I re-visited Germany on holiday and went to see the German family with whom I had spent an extremely happy summer in 1930, in Heidelberg, and at their holiday home in the Bavarian Alps. I had been back briefly in 1931 and again in 1934, but in 1936 I was shocked to find the extent to which Hitler had acquired control not only of the German Reich but also of the hearts and minds of the German people. The head of the German family in Heidelberg was Klara Burger von Duhn [*a daughter of the late Professor Friedrich von Duhn*], a member of a well-known and respected University family, and also a delightfully intelligent and tolerant person, who made no bones about pulling the leg of her younger son, Till, aged about 17, about his enthusiasm for the 'brown shirts', who were then – in 1930 – generally regarded as something of a joke. By 1936, however, Till was a fully-fledged member of the Nazi organisation and even his broad-minded and tolerant mother was admitting that the Nazis 'had something' and was herself doing voluntary work within the various Nazi womens' organisations.

'The writing on the wall' therefore seemed to me to spell out clearly that there was trouble to come and, as soon as I got home to England, I joined a Territorial Army Anti-Aircraft Battery with their HQ in Barnes. It was however only a matter of three months before I received a summons to Head Office of my employers, Sun Insurance Office Ltd, offering me a posting to the 'Sun' Branch in Shanghai – an offer at which I jumped, as, after 3 years in a London office, I was by then contemplating resigning from the 'Sun' and enlisting in the ranks. So it was that at the beginning of March 1937 I travelled overland to Marseilles to join the P&O liner RMS *RAJPUTANA*, having first taken the precaution of joining the Regular Army Reserve of Officers – this on the strength of Certificate 'A' in the OTC at Harrow, but not on account of 3 months service as Gunner Laird in a TA Ack-Ack Battery!

On arrival in Shanghai at the beginning of April 1937 I found myself in a completely different world – particularly in the social environment in which I now found myself: a beer-drinking fell fox-hunter [*my father had for many years hunted on foot with the Coniston and Blencathra fell foxhound packs in the Lake District*] and/

or motor cyclist like myself was a complete 'fish out of water' in the 'balls, picnics and parties' social round of Shanghai. Feeling that I must acquire some basic skill in the art of 'ball dancing' I answered a newspaper advertisement for dancing lessons, but that did not last long when I found that my instructor was a rather unattractive Russian male; so I resorted to practising my skills (or lack of them) on the dance floor by going to a nearby cabaret and dancing school with a Chinese taxi-dancer, an attractive, and probably very young, girl who was very patient and helped me to build up a little self-confidence.

It did not take me long to realise that Shanghai was a place of immense possibilities, and having joined the Shanghai Cricket Club and the Race Club (both just across the road from the China United Apartments where I was living) I found I was easily able to get a game of Cricket (at my level), and at the Race Club a game of Squash – initially with a Chinese 'marker' who, like all their breed, were experts at giving one a game at, or slightly above, one's own level. I had also acquired the loan of a pony from someone who was on leave, which I kept at a Riding School at Hunjon alongside the railway which ran round the International Settlement and was outside the Settlement boundary. I used to ride out on a bicycle (slightly unusual behaviour for Europeans) to the Riding School in the early morning, but never attained any real proficiency on horseback despite the efforts of a charming Russian ex-cavalry officer. I felt sorry for the pony having to submit to my unskilled efforts and often wondered what became of the Riding School and its owner and the ponies in the schemozzle (Sino-Japanese war) which blew up very shortly afterwards.

[*Letter from Richard to his sister Maudie*]

China United Apartments
28 June 1937

My Dear Maudie
    This is, I fear, long overdue, but I seem to spend a large proportion of my time writing letters and am never up to date with them.

So far we have been blessed with a remarkably cool summer, but it is beginning to warm up now and get into the state of damp stickiness for which Shanghai seems to be quite famous. However we are fairly lucky here as it does not last more than two or three months, whilst in Hong Kong it seems to be more or less a permanency.

Life is now proceeding very rapidly and smoothly here. I don't as yet know a vast number of people but quite enough to prevent me getting bored and I have no doubt that by the time I am due for home leave I shall know a great deal more than is good for my friend Mr Barclay (of banking, not brewing, fame). My life here up to date has been a very bachelor one and my pleasures taken in a very bachelor manner. One has however to be rather circumspect in one's actions as the British community is sufficiently small to take an active and not altogether welcome interest in the 'goings-on' of its members. Apart from that Shanghai has much to recommend it and I find it preferable to London as a place to work. One can live very well indeed for comparatively little money but it is apt to become expensive when one starts going out to amuse oneself. Riding is very cheap: at the moment I am keeping a pony for another bloke which costs me 40 dollars a month – at the moment the dollar is worth one and tuppence halfpenny – and that is the sum total of my expenses as far as riding is concerned: if one rides regularly it is well worth while. The more energetic gentlemen get up and ride every morning before breakfast, but most of them keep their ponies at the Race Club, which is just across the road from here. As a result their riding is limited to the racecourse as it is a good 3 to 4 miles to the outskirts of the town. The racecourse is all very fine if one happens to have a race pony in training, but it is not much 'cop' otherwise. It takes me a good 20 minutes of hard pedalling on my bike to get to the place where I keep my pony. I am disinclined to take a taxi each time, and I have not got enough cash to buy a motor car, so it would mean getting up at about 5 a.m. if I was to have a ride and be at the office by 8.30.

I generally play tennis about three times a week and ride the other evenings and at weekends, so all things being considered I am fitter than for many years past. For tennis I have joined the Cricket Club which sounds a bit Irish but they have got some of the best courts in Shanghai: it is a British club and reasonably cheap. The centre of the racecourse, where the Cricket Club is situated, is one of the few centrally located open places in Shanghai and is therefore the centre of the most terrific activity of the sporting nature in the evenings. There are about four cricket clubs, umpteen tennis clubs, a polo club and a baseball club.

There is an awful lot of poverty in Shanghai and, as generally happens when you get the extremes of poverty and wealth living more or less alongside each other, there is a lot of crime, very often accompanied by violence. One seems to read practically every day in the paper of affrays between the police and armed robbers and bandits. It is generally the wealthy Chinese whom they try to rob as they have a much bigger share of the wealth of Shanghai than the foreigner, and they do not treat the people who work for them nearly as well.

The Settlement Police are a rather fine lot of blokes and furthermore have to be pretty tough as there are quite a number of casualties amongst them each year. Most of the ordinary constables are Chinese, who are all men of much better physique than the average Chinaman: there is a considerable sprinkling of Sikhs, big fine looking men with beards who are most impressive to look at. Some of the NCOs are Sikhs, some are British and some are Russian. I think the British are on a different footing to the others and can work up to commissions if they want; as far as I know all the officers are British. They have things pretty well taped for dealing with any trouble. There is what is known as the 'Riot Squad' who are always standing by and who are rushed to the scene of any trouble. This seems to happen at least once a week, so beneath the veneer of wealth and prosperity of a somewhat garish nature things are not as happy as they might be. It seems to be a fairly normal state of affairs in the East, as if the Chinese cannot get what they want by peaceful means they are apt to get violent, and have to be dealt with in kind.

By far the largest foreign community in Shanghai is Russian: a big batch of refugees came down here after the Revolution, but there are a lot more coming in now from Harbin as economically

Manchuria has gone all to pot since the Japanese took it over. Most of them (the Russians) are very poor and don't seem to have much enterprise. Some of the girls are very pretty, but one of their great ambitions is to entrap an unwary Englishman into marrying them and so get his nationality, all of which makes them a little dangerous. Englishmen are their favourite target as it is only under British law that the wife automatically takes the nationality of her husband. The place where I keep my pony is run by a Russian, an ex-cavalry officer, who still flies the old Imperial flag over his stables, and who is a most charming and interesting person to talk to. The White Russians were fighting right up to 1920, poor devils, which one never seems to realise.

I have almost given up worrying about what is happening in Europe, not because I am so far away, but because Hitler and Mussolini between them seem to be giving such a perfect lesson in how not to be diplomatic that one just kind of shuts one's eyes and hopes for the best. It would be a good thing if they and all their satellites could die a nice quiet natural death – it would cause too much of an upset if they were to be 'bumped off' too violently. The more one thinks about it the more depressed one gets which does not help anybody, so it seems easier to take the lazy way out and not think about it. Maybe too many of us are thinking like that, in which case we may all pay for it later.

Am sending this to 'Tarn Rigg' as I don't quite know where you are just now. Are there any prospects of Colin getting a job on the China Station or does the Q.E. appointment last for many moons yet. [*Lieutenant Commander Colin Gatey, Maudie's naval officer husband, was the Senior Engineer on the battleship* HMS *Queen Elizabeth.*]

Must stop now: remember me to the family.

V. much love, Richard

So, by the beginning of August 1937 I was beginning to find my feet when a Sino-Japanese 'incident', which had started at the Marco Polo Bridge near Peking [*Beijing*] at the beginning of July, spread down to the Shanghai area and threatened to involve the International Settlement. This did indeed become a reality when as a result of an 'incident' involving a couple of Japanese servicemen on one of the 'outside' roads (ie a road outside the International Settlement) the Chinese Army, who were present in considerable strength in the areas around Shanghai, decided to do something about it – ie to try and push the Japanese into the sea, or more accurately the Whampoa River [*the Huangpu River*]. Shanghai was not unused to 'flaps' of this kind and during a fairly hectic 'Poker Dice' session at the Shanghai Cricket Club I allowed myself with the gentlest persuasion to be enrolled in the Scottish Company of the Shanghai Volunteer Corps (S.V.C.). The name of Laird and the fact of Scottish descent (as opposed to Scottish birth) proved to be no obstacle. Two days later the Volunteers were mobilised and the Shanghai Scottish, together with A Company – our 'English' opposite numbers – were sent up to their allotted sector of the International Settlement boundary. This was immediately opposite Shanghai's Main Railway Station (the North Station – just inside Chinese territory) and from the experience of previous 'troubles' known as 'Windy Corner'. We were based in a Chinese school (Elgin Road School) and were responsible for manning three or four road crossings into Chinese territory protected by sandbag emplacements and heavy iron gates – the latter designed to try and control refugees trying to get into the Settlement rather than to stop any military attempt to force entry into the Settlement.

The Japanese appeared to have been rather taken by surprise by the Chinese moves and at that time the only troops that they had in the area were about 4,000 Japanese Marines (Japanese Naval Landing Party), against a vastly superior force of Chinese (said to be some of their better divisions). The Japanese did however have the benefit of support of naval gunfire from their ships in the Whampoa River. The Chinese were firmly in control of the North Station at this time and the Japanese were busy shelling them from their ships in the River, and with mortars and field artillery. This was mostly fairly small calibre stuff, which was fortunate for us as quite a number of shells fell on our side of the Settlement boundary, doing some damage to the Chinese shop-houses near us but fortunately without causing any casualties to us (although I did collect some nice pieces of shell as souvenirs). A sidelight on the strange situation which existed in Shanghai was that the Japanese were members of the International Settlement, and even had a Japanese Company which was part of the Shanghai Volunteer Corps. When therefore Japanese shells started falling on our side of the Settlement boundary it was possible to ring up the Japanese Coy of the S.V.C. and ask them to get their ships to correct their aim: we were in fact doing their spotting for them! Another sidelight on the rather strange situation which existed in Shanghai was that the districts of Hongkou and Yangtszepoo, nominally part of the International Settlement, were by now effectively under Japanese control, and did indeed form the base from which the Japanese later took the offensive to drive the Chinese forces out of the areas around Shanghai.

During the 48 hours we were at 'Windy Corner' there was thought to be a distinct possibility that the Chinese would try to force their way into the Settlement in order to take the Japanese in the flank. The atmosphere was therefore decidedly tense as there was little we could effectively have done to stop the Chinese if they had really decided to make a move; in fact our orders were merely to make a token show of resistance. Another vivid impression of 'Windy Corner' was the noise made by the bursting of even small calibre shells – made worse, no doubt, by the fact that they were bursting in narrow streets. However, one did surprisingly quickly get accustomed to the idea that with this sort of shell-fire its bark was worse than its bite. It was at this time that a colleague of mine who had been landed with the job of looking after the office sent a cable off to Head Office about the welfare of members of staff which included the report 'Laird in action with the Volunteers', which caused some unjustified alarm at home.

After the first 48 hours or so, reinforcements of Regular Troops arrived from Hong Kong and they and/or the Shanghai Municipal

Council's 'Russian Regiment' took over our positions, whilst we went back to billets in the Race Club from where we were deployed on internal security duties helping the Police. These duties kept us busy but were not unduly onerous. Our living conditions at the Race Club were good; we got a free ration of beer every day, a little time off to play cricket and a free cinema show three times a week (the horrors of war!!) – this at a time when all the cinemas in the Settlement were closed.

The closure of all places of public entertainment followed the so-called 'Bloody Saturday' bombings on Saturday 14th August 1937. These bombings were in fact air raids by the Chinese Air Force who, in monsoon weather (low cloud and strong winds) were trying to bomb HIJNS *IDZUMO*, an old Japanese cruiser acting as guard ship moored near the Japanese Consulate downstream from the junction of the Soochow Creek with the Whampoa River. [*HIJNS* IZUMO, *or* IDZUMO, *was a Japanese armoured cruiser built in the late 1890s in Britain by Armstrong Whitworth. She was actively involved in the Russo-Japanese War 1904-05, the First World War, the Sino-Japanese War in Shanghai in 1937, and in the Second World War. She was eventually sunk by American carrier-borne aircraft in July 1945.*] One bomb (or bombs) fell outside the Cathay Hotel in Nanking Road near its junction with The Bund, while the other bomb (or bombs) fell in the middle of the very busy Great World cross-roads near the Race Course. Both Nanking Road and, particularly, the Great World cross-roads were very crowded at the time (nearly all Chinese) and these bombs were reported to have caused 700 and 1000 deaths respectively. It was assumed that the Nanking Road bomb was a bad shot for the *IDZUMO*. The Great World bomb was a considerable distance from the *IDZUMO* and it is thought that the plane which dropped it might have been hit by anti-aircraft fire and was trying to shed its bomb onto the Race Course which was the only open space available, and a very short distance from the Great World crossing. These very heavy casualties came as a great shock to all the people of Shanghai – if only because at the time nobody knew how this bout of Sino-Japanese 'trouble' was going to develop. Some units of the Shanghai Volunteer Corps (S.V.C.) – including several friends in the Armoured Car Company – were called out to help in the grim job of clearing up the casualties at the Great World, but the 'Scottish' fortunately missed out on this as we were otherwise engaged at 'Windy Corner'.

Bobbie [*his future wife*] (whom I did not at the time know, although I did know her by sight (her father, Dr Harry Couper Patrick was the M.O. [*Medical Officer*] to the Shanghai Scottish) was also uncomfortably close to the events of 'Bloody Saturday'. The office in which she worked was in the same building as the Cathay Hotel; she had been in the office on that Saturday morning and the bombing happened in the early afternoon. She had gone back home from the office – home being on the north side of the Soochow Creek close to the Japanese Consulate and the *IDZUMO*'s berth. During the next day or two she got a grandstand, and uncomfortably close, view of further attempts to bomb or torpedo the *IDZUMO*. One torpedo (from an M.T.B.) hit the wharf close to where the *IDZUMO* was lying causing a terrific explosion.

Shortly after this the British Authorities decided that, as the situation was still decidedly uncertain, as many British women and children as possible should be 'encouraged' (ie at their own expense) to leave Shanghai. Among those who left, with some misgivings, were Bobbie and her mother, by destroyer (HMS *DAINTY*) to Woosung at the junction of the Whampoa with the Yangtze and thence on the *EMPRESS OF ASIA* ('Steerage class!!') to Hong Kong, where the welcome for the evacuees was not exactly enthusiastic. Nor did prices for accommodation in Hong Kong seem very fair to evacuees who had been pressurised into leaving Shanghai taking only what they could carry. The general reaction was that 'The Colony' had lived up to its reputation for 'stickiness' compared to cosmopolitan Shanghai.

Reverting to our internal security duties after being withdrawn from 'Windy Corner', these consisted of supporting the Police on foot patrols and helping to supervise the distribution of food supplies, which for a time immediately after the outbreak of hostilities were very scarce. Another job was guarding the compound where civilian employees of a large Japanese cotton mill lived – quite a necessary precaution as there was very strong anti-Japanese feeling among the surrounding Chinese population. The Japanese cotton mill employees were genuinely glad to have us around and made sure we had unlimited supplies of beer – no bad thing as this was at the height of the Shanghai summer with temperatures well up in the 90s Fahrenheit – very de-hydrating!! The least pleasant internal security job (fortunately only one day of it) was guarding the bridges over the Soochow Creek – the 'Creek' being in fact a tidal tributary of the Whampoa River about 30 to 40 yards wide. At the time it had a large number of corpses of men, women, children and animals in it which were neither pleasant to behold or to smell. Some of them were terribly mutilated, and they all became bloated and horrible from the heat of the sun as they came to and from on each tide.

At the end of August/early September after about three weeks of 'active service' the Volunteers were stood down and returned to their civilian jobs in offices etc, but for a time we still used to go to work in uniform with our rifles and equipment in case we were required to turn out at short notice. This did not arise, but heavy fighting continued around the Settlement until mid-November. The Chinese, having at one stage come close to pushing the Japanese into the river, were finally forced to withdraw as Japanese reinforcements were landed at Woosung and eventually joined up with the Japanese Naval landing party who had been pinned down in the Hongkew sector of the Settlement. During this time we in the Settlement were 'entertained' by Japanese bombing raids on Chinese positions near the North Station and Chinese bombing raids on Japanese ships in the river, who put up spectacular barrages of anti-aircraft fire. I was at the time living in the China United Apartments (CUA), a 9 to 10 storey apartment block, from the

Dining Room of which on the top floor one got a panoramic view across to the North Station and Chapei. From here – conveniently at breakfast time – one could watch the daily Japanese bombing of my old friend the North Station. The bombs, clearly visible to the naked eye, leaving the planes quite slowly at first and then falling so quickly that the eye could no longer follow them.

Before the Chinese finally withdrew they carried out a 'scorched earth' policy and set fire to Chapei (a Chinese area to the north of the Settlement) and to Pootung on the other side of the river. [*Now Pudong – the site of stunning high-rise developments including the Oriental Pearl Tower, the Shanghai World Financial Center, the Jinmao Tower and the Shanghai Tower.*] For days Chapei seen from the CUA was a solid wall of smoke by day, and by night was luridly lit up by the fires underneath. One Chinese 'stay behind' unit of about 500 men did however establish themselves in a big reinforced concrete godown [*warehouse*] just inside Chapei and clearly visible from the CUA – maybe a quarter of a mile away. They held out for four days and then one night the Japs opened up on the godown with field guns at point blank range: the two sides of the godown, one of them facing towards the CUA, had windows but the end walls were blank. The Japs were firing at the blank walls and it was so close that you could see the impact of the shells on the wall and then, through the windows in the side, the explosion of the shell burst inside – horrible, but fascinating to watch. One wondered how anything could live inside, but after about an hour's shelling some of the goods stored in the godown caught fire and the Chinese came out. They had a small gap to cover between their godown and the British lines on the Settlement boundary, but although the Japs had a searchlight and a machine gun trained on the gap, 370 men got across with only two casualties. Apparently they came across one at a time and let the Japs waste their ammunition; there was a British officer so close that he could hear the Japs changing the belts on their machine gun and gave the Chinese the tip so that a whole batch of them could get across unmolested.

On Armistice Day (1937) the British and American warships in the river (HMS *SUFFOLK*, and USS *AUGUSTA*) were dressed overall for the occasion, but against a solid background of smoke and flames from the burning buildings in Pootung – no Armistice there!! It was to this scene that Bobbie returned from Hongkong and came for a time to live at the CUA. I soon found out who this attractive girl was who joined the rest of the residents of the CUA watching the fires in Chapei from the Dining Room. Moreover, she further impressed me by walking through the throngs of Chinese down Nanking Road wearing a leopard-skin coat – Europeans, particularly European girls, not being generally given to walking to their offices. But I remained much too shy as a newcomer to Shanghai to dare to approach a long-standing Shanghai resident such as Bobbie. It was to be nearly three years before I did meet her 'officially'.

Once the actual fighting moved away from the neighbourhood of Shanghai, life in the Settlement, at least for the Europeans, returned more or less to normal with the active social and sporting life for which Shanghai was well known and which the 'Shanghailanders' were reluctant to give up. There were however limitations; the country areas around Shanghai were still effectively under Japanese control and excursions outside the Settlement boundaries could easily lead to unpleasant 'incidents'. There were still numbers of unburied corpses around, and for a time the Chinese peasants were reluctant to return to their land to cultivate it because the Japanese were so unpredictable in their reactions. Travel up-country on business (something I had greatly looked forward to) was virtually out of the question. All that I did see of China proper was on two brief weekend trips before the 'trouble' started – one to Hangchow and one to Wusih. Even the Hongkew and Yangtzepoo sectors of the International Settlement north of the Soochow Creek were under Japanese control and access to them was severely restricted. This Bobbie knew to her cost, because her parents had had to evacuate their house in Whampoa

Road near the Japanese Consulate and had moved into a flat at the Shanghai General Hospital (on the north bank of the Creek) where her father was Resident Medical Superintendent. Despite holding an official Japanese Pass, access north of the Creek was not allowed during the hours of curfew (a situation which Bobbie had to allow for in making her social arrangements) and from time to time the bridges over the Creek would be closed without warning if there had been an 'incident'.

[*Letter from Richard to his sister Maudie*]

China United Apartments
22 October 1937

My dear Maudie

Much water seems to have flowed under the bridges since I got your letter and I apologise for not having written before now. I believe you were staying with H & B [*their brother Henry and wife Barbie*] at the time that the real bother started in Shanghai, so you probably got all the various rumours about me being 'in action' or evacuated to Hong Kong etc. Needless to say, none of them were true and I was blissfully ignorant of all such excitements until I returned to civilian life at the end of August. In fact the whole affair seems to have been taken far more seriously by the outside world than by Shanghai itself. For a few days we all felt ourselves rather in the centre of the news, and in a certain physical danger, which led to some rather highly coloured reports being circulated to the outside world. Also, Shanghai is a very peculiar place with large native cities under Chinese control on either side of the French Concession and the International Settlement. The Settlement itself is divided into two sections by the Soochow Creek, a tributary of the main river, the Whampoa, which in its turn flows into the Yangtze Kiang about 15/20 miles away. Soochow Creek is itself 30 or 40 yards wide, in other words quite a respectable river, albeit of the sluggish, muddy and odiferous variety which is all that they know as rivers in this part of China. North of Soochow Creek is the part of the Settlement where most of the Japanese live, but of course in normal times the bulk of the population is Chinese and there are also a few other foreigners. It is also the district where many of the large foreign-owned factories and warehouses are situated. Except for one comparatively small corner, which is held by British troops, all the Settlement north of Soochow Creek is now absolutely under the control of the Japanese military authorities. Most of the Chinese and foreigners evacuated in the early days of the trouble.

For the first few days the Japanese were very hard pressed; they only had 4,000 men against about ten times that number of Chinese, and furthermore Chinese snipers were giving them pretty good hell from the rear. The result was that they shot any Chinese on sight; it sounds pretty brutal and a lot of innocent people were killed. Some of the Settlement Police who were down there all the time say that many Chinese died of starvation in their houses as they knew they would be shot if they went outside. Later on, when things were not so critical, the Japs rather showed their true colours. If they thought there was a sniper in a given house, they would set the whole row alight, catch anybody who came out and then shoot or bayonet them in cold blood.

When the Japanese officer and Marine got shot up at the aerodrome outside Shanghai (that was the incident which started up the Trouble down here) everybody thought that the Japs had done it on purpose just to make trouble. However in view of the fact that they were so badly outnumbered during the first few days of the fighting, it looks rather as if the Chinese chose to make their big effort down here.

On the other hand they ought to be ashamed of themselves that they did not push the Japs into the river during those early days. Thank heaven they did not, as there would have been a massacre of Japanese civilians, and the Chinese troops would probably have tried to break into the Settlement south of the Soochow Creek. I am afraid they would have succeeded too, as at that time no reinforcements had arrived from Hong Kong and we only had one British battalion, one battalion of American Marines and the SVC. The SVC is about 2,000 strong, but by the time you have deducted the Chinese and Japanese Companies and the other odds and sods, you could not rely on more than about one battalion who would try to put up as good a show as possible. All that lot, 3 battalions in all, had a front of about 10 miles to hold, so that things were pretty critical in those early days. As is so often the case, the real crisis was over by the time the reinforcements arrived. Whether things will get bad again is hard to say. At the moment the Japs are trying to drive a wedge into the Chinese lines, to separate the troops in the immediate neighbourhood of Shanghai from the rest. If they succeed in doing that the Chinese near Shanghai will be fighting with their backs to the Settlement, instead of with one flank resting on it as at the moment, and then things could become uncomfortable for us again. From a military point of view the Chinese have got very little to gain by hanging on to Chapei, the native city on the north of the International Settlement boundary, but I think they are very afraid of losing face with their own people if they retire. The obvious thing is for them to retire up-country to get out of range of the Japanese naval guns, and at the same time lengthen the Japanese lines of communication.

Once the fighting moves away, Shanghai will be able to recover itself a bit, but at the moment business is as near dead as it can be. What will be the future of Shanghai is very hard to say; it probably depends on what sort of a treaty the Chinese are able to make with the Japanese to finish their 'war'. I think it was the Chinese who elected to have a scrap down here, and all the damage and loss of life which has happened in the Settlement would not have taken place but for that decision. After the 1932 'Trouble' there was supposed to be a de-militarised zone around Shanghai, but during the past 18 months or so that has been consistently broken by the Chinese. Until a few days before the outbreak of this 'war' they did not have many troops in that zone (they were supposed to have none at all), but they have been pretty busy for some time past building concrete pill-boxes. These, most conveniently, can be disguised as grave mounds, and it is undoubtedly these long-prepared positions which have enabled them to put up such a fight. Another advantage for them in choosing to put up their main resistance down here is that their communications and lines of supply are much shorter and better. Furthermore the country is very flat and in wet weather very marshy; in fact it is normally paddy fields, and is broken up in all directions by a maze of creeks, great and small. In such country the Japanese lose much of the advantage which the greater mechanization of their army would otherwise give them, so the Chinese were no fools in starting up down here, although it was most unfortunate for Shanghai. There was also always the chance that the foreign powers would somehow get involved, owing to the presence of the foreign concessions. Most of the Chinese I have spoken to would frankly have been very glad to see that, and yet in the unlikely event of their winning the war the first thing they would want to do would be to abolish the extra-territorial rights.

There has been a lot of nonsense talked about the deliberate bombing of civilians by the Japs, but if there has been any at all I think it has been grossly exaggerated by the Chinese in an attempt to increase sympathy for their cause. A village three or four miles outside Shanghai was bombed recently and there were a number of civilian casualties. There was immediately a terrific outcry in the local pro-Chinese press and Chinese military authorities said there were no troops within miles, whilst the Japs denied this. As a matter of curiosity I went out riding there myself a few days later and found the whole countryside lousy with small detachments of Chinese soldiers. Also that particular village happened to be close to a strategic river bridge and the whole area was surrounded by trenches and sandbag redoubts. I have no doubt that if one were to investigate, one would find similar conditions in 99% of the places where there have been civilian casualties. Another thing that this 'war' has shown up is that aerial bombing, anyway as practised by the oriental nations, is very far from being a deadly accurate form of bombardment. The Chinese themselves gave a pretty convincing demonstration of that on August 14th, or 'Bloody Saturday' as it is known here, when they killed or wounded some 2,000 of their own people on neutral territory. Although nearly all the aerial bombardment since then has been done by the Japs, only about one tenth or less of the total casualties in the Settlement have been caused by Japanese bombs. To the best of my knowledge only two Japanese bombs have fallen inside the Settlement boundary and caused casualties, and they were only inside by about 70 yards, as compared to the average half a mile for the Chinese. Whilst I sympathise with the Chinese in the defence of their country, I do dislike their 'injured innocence' attitude over this particular issue. Their planes never come over in daylight now as they have undoubtedly lost a good many, a lot of which have probably been destroyed on the ground as their landing fields have been pretty thoroughly bombed. Their night raids seem singularly ineffective as they drop their bombs indiscriminately from a great height on the area occupied by the Japanese. The military value of such bombing seems to be nil, and they generally succeed only in setting fire to Chinese owned property in that area. The Japanese warships down river put up a terrific barrage of anti-aircraft fire which never seems to bring a plane down, but it does have the effect of keeping them much too high to be able to do any accurate bombing; it is also quite pretty to watch with the searchlights and tracer shells. One does not however want to stick one's head too far out of the window, as every now and then one hears the spent shrapnel come whistling past the window.

Although it seemed pretty exciting at the time my own part in this do was really a very small one. The British troops in our sector now are having a very much worse time than we ever did as the fighting is much more severe. Also, when we were there the Japs had no planes other than a couple of seaplanes belonging to their flagship, so there was no aerial bombardment of the North Station which is now a regular performance. One thing in their favour is that their posts are very much stronger than when we were there; at first there were no roofs and, although we managed to build temporary ones, they would not have kept much out.

When I first came out here, I decided that I had better join an infantry unit, and partly as a result of an alcoholic evening with a Scotsman, I joined the Shanghai Scottish, of which I am really glad as they seem a nice lot. The day after we were mobilised we went to our posts on the Settlement boundary, at 'Windy Corner'. It was, and still is, one of the more exciting spots on the Settlement boundary as it juts out into Chinese territory. Also the Japanese front line comes right up to the Settlement boundary on one flank of the sector, so that we were apt to 'cop' it from both sides. It was quite frightening when either side was doing a bombardment, but very much more so when the Chinese were busy as they really were most erratic and narrowly missed hitting two of our posts, quite apart from the many shells which they put well inside the Settlement. The Japs were at least consistent and more accurate.

Being a slightly blood-thirsty individual I must say I thoroughly enjoyed the time we were mobilised and after the heat of summer in an office the open air life was a grand change. Our grub was good, we had no worries unless we chose to imagine them, and discipline was not unduly harsh. For married people, of course, it was not so funny; the evacuation of women and children was made as near compulsory as possible without the authorities having to pay for it. It was probably quite right that they should go as even now Shanghai is far from being an ideal place, but some people have been pretty hard hit by having to run one home in Shanghai and one in Hong Kong. I believe that the prices for accommodation in Hong Kong went up to the skies; I think that the least the authorities could have done was to see that the 'evacuees' were not made the victims of profiteers. Many of them would have preferred to have stayed in Shanghai, but left nevertheless as they were more or less told that they would be 'un public spirited' if they stayed, yet they seem to have had a pretty raw deal in return for their 'public spiritedness'. There was a certain amount of unwarranted grousing, but on balance Hong Kong seems to have lived up to the reputation for 'stickiness' which it enjoys in Shanghai.

I don't quite know when this will get to you; it will have to go to Hong Kong by local steamer and wait for a mail from there. The Siberian route is working, and seems to be all right for printed stuff, such as papers, but not so good for letters (which probably means that the b_____s are taking a look at them).

Please remember me to the family.

V. much love, Richard

[*Letter from Richard to his sister Maudie*]

c/o Sun Insurance Office,
1 the Bund
24 April 1938

My Dear Maudie,

I fear it is a very long time ago now since I got your letter.

The Japanese policy at the moment is to keep all areas under their control closed to foreigners, undoubtedly with the intention of crippling foreign trade for good. Thus, while they allow their own merchant ships to go up the Yangtze, with that tender regard for other people's interests for which they have won such a notable reputation, they refuse to allow the ships of other nations to use the river on the grounds of danger from mines floated down by the Chinese. There is talk now of organising weekly convoys of British ships, for we have after all got exactly the same right to use the Yangtze as they have.

Another example of their policy of obstruction is their refusal to open up that part of the Settlement which is at present occupied by their army. Most of the big factories are in that area, and an enormous amount of money is being lost merely because firms are unable to resume normal working conditions. Some of them are working on a reduced scale and all Chinese employees have to have passes. Many of them have to walk 3 or 4 miles to their work as there are still no buses, trams or rickshaws over there, and they are not allowed bicycles. The other day a Chinese employee of the BAT [*British American Tobacco*] was stopped for his pass which was perfectly in order, but he was detained for the whole day until a foreign employee of BAT managed to bail him out. The Chinaman's only offence was that he had had his photograph for the pass taken with his hat on, so when the sentry (who regards himself almost as the personification of the Emperor, or at any rate as his direct and personal representative) looked at the pass, the Chinese was in effect looking at the Emperor of Japan without doffing his hat – an unpardonable offence. That at any rate is the Japanese argument. That is the sort of thing we have to put up with.

At the beginning of hostilities the Japanese confiscated all the dredgers and other vessels belonging to the Whampoa Conservancy Board, and since then they have refused to let them do any maintenance work on the river, which brings down a lot of silt; people are getting very worried as to what will happen if they don't do some dredging in the near future.

Now that we have no more fighting in the immediate neighbourhood of Shanghai life is very quiet here. We still have two battalions of troops here instead of the usual one; the permanent battalion is one of the Durham Light Infantry, and the extra one is a battalion of Seaforth Highlanders from Hong Kong.

We are still more or less confined to the limits of the settlement and the French Concession. If one does go out into the country one has to take into consideration the possibility of coming across some drunken Japanese soldier, who may take it into his head to be unpleasant. There have been one or two rather nasty incidents in which foreign women were involved, and it certainly does not seem to be safe for a girl to go out beyond the railway unless she has at least two men with her. The stories one hears about the raping of Chinese women are 'summat awful', so that it is no wonder that the farmers are reluctant to go back to their land. All of which is rather serious as it means that this year's rice crop is not being planted. There was quite a serious shortage last winter and it looks as though it may be even worse this coming winter. The discipline in the Japanese Army seems to be appalling, which in my view accounts for many of the various incidents and lootings that one hears of. I think that most of the troops around Shanghai have been on active service for some months and are sent down here for a rest as this is a quiet sector. There is no doubt about it that actual fighting does have a brutalising effect on men, and unless your discipline is pretty strict the troops very soon get out of hand, which is what seems to have been happening with the Japs.

I moved away from the China United Apartments at the beginning of this month and have now got a house of my own – a single room flat, which I like very much better. I have a 'boy' who cooks for me, cleans the flat and generally looks after me. I only have to pay him $25 per month (about 30 shillings) and he seems to be reasonably honest. He buys all the food in the market and gets any other odd things I may require, so he probably gets his little bit of 'squeeze' on all such transactions. As long as you don't let the 'squeeze' racket get out of hand it does not matter, in fact in a way it is a good thing for if you supervise a boy so strictly that he cannot get something for himself, he gets his own back by being lazy.

I don't know whether this will get to you in time for your birthday, but anyway many happy returns to you Maudie.

Much love, Richard

In September 1938 I was lucky enough to be allowed to take three weeks local leave for a holiday in the Diamond Mountains [*Kumgangsan, or Mount Kumgang*] in what is now North Korea. For this I had to thank my boss in Shanghai (Pat Pottinger) who authorised this leave on the grounds that since my arrival in Shanghai in April 1937 I had not had a break, even though I had been through the 'war' (notwithstanding the fact that I regarded the time that I was mobilised in the Volunteers as an excellent break from office routine!!). Anyway, off we went to Korea – a party of four, two blokes and two girls. Myself and one of the girls (Edith Palmer) were supposedly chaperones to the other pair – my chum Ian Aucott [*subsequently my godfather*] and his girlfriend, Mai-mai Ross.

We crossed from Shanghai to Nagasaki on one of the regular Japanese steamers on that route (a 24 hour crossing). She was a very reasonable Cross-Channel type of ship, but then I later discovered that she had been built by Denny's of Dumbarton, where in years gone by my father had served his shipbuilding apprenticeship. What put me on this line of enquiry was the fact that all the 'loos' on the ship were made by 'Shanks of Barrhead' – quite like home! On this ship we got our first taste of Japanese officialdom which was to be with us for the whole of the rest of the trip except for 14 days or so when we were in our holiday area in the Diamond Mountains. Starting on the ship we had to submit stools for examination by the ship's doctor (specimens induced by an enema administered by the ship's doctor if a specimen could not be produced on demand). [*This was because of a cholera scare in Japan at the time.*] Any books that we had with us had to be approved by the Japanese

Customs, who impounded any books or magazines thought likely to corrupt the morals of the Japanese people; the impounded books were handed back to us on our return to Nagasaki on our way back to Shanghai. One bloke from Shanghai on the ship was an ardent member of the Armoured Car Company of the SVC, and had with him a couple of Armoured Car Training Manuals for his holiday reading; these were not of the slightest interest to the Japanese (they probably had their own copies anyway)!

Our journey to the Diamond Mountains took us by train through attractive hilly countryside to Shimonoseki, followed by a night sea crossing to Fusan at the southern tip of the Korean Peninsula and then by train to Keijo (now Seoul) the capital of Korea. There we spent a night in the principal hotel in the town – a rather grim pile, enlivened only by the presence of a party of British and Australian gold miners (including the well-known character 'One Arm Sutton' – an old Etonian). [*Major General Francis 'Frank' Arthur Sutton MC who lost an arm at Gallipoli. After leaving the army he became an adventurer, and at various times builder of railways and a gold miner. He became a general to the Chinese warlord Zhang Zuolin, and died in internment in Hong Kong in 1944.*] These characters had been working on gold dredges on the Amur River on the borders of Manchuria and Russia and had managed to amass sizeable quantities of gold which they had got as far as Keijo. Here the Japanese had refused to allow them to leave the country unless they left their gold behind. This they refused to do and when we saw them they were busy drinking and gambling their way through their stock of gold; I never heard what happened to them in the end.

The Japanese had by this time (September 1938) been at war in China for over a year and were extremely suspicious of foreigners, whose movements were watched very carefully. On trains and boats we were asked a standard set of questions (some of them seemingly quite irrelevant), the answers to which were passed on to the next sector, where the official for that sector asked us the same set of questions and woe betide us if there were any discrepancies in our answers. The reaction was every bit as bad if the Japanese had made any errors (not unknown!) in transmitting our replies from one sector to the next.

From Keijo we went in a small electric train through some spectacular mountain scenery. The steeper sections were surmounted by a series of zig-zags; at the end of each 'zig' and each 'zag' was an extended siding along the mountainside into which the train (2 or 3 coaches only) went forwards and, the points having been switched, came out backwards and up the next section of line; and so on until the top of the pass was reached (a system of surmounting gradients which I have not seen elsewhere).

The Chosen (Korean) Government Railways had established two small tourist hotels, one on the western side of the Diamond Mountains and one on the east, both inside what is now North Korea. These hotels were very adequate and catered to some extent for European tastes. We spent the first week in the hotel on the western side of the mountains, walking through beautiful mountain scenery and bathing in the mountain streams, some of which had lovely deep, clear and rather cold pools. After the heat of a Shanghai summer this holiday in the mountains was wonderfully refreshing – wood fires in the lounge in the evening and blankets on the bed at night. We bathed Japanese style (but not mixed!) in the large square baths – about 8 feet square and 2 foot 6 inches deep and full of beautifully hot water – marvellously refreshing after a hard day's walking in the mountains.

At the end of the first week we walked over the mountains to the hotel near the east coast, stopping a night on the way at an Alpine-style hut on the ridge of the main range. Here we met a very pleasant and good-looking junior official from the Italian Embassy in Tokyo who rather fancied himself with the girls in the party (not reciprocated!). His name for some reason has stuck, Count Stefano Macchi di Cellere; I have often wondered what became of him. [*This is believed to be the son of Count Vincenzo*

Macchi di Cellere, Italian ambassador to Argentina 1907 to 1912 and subsequently Italian Ambassador to the United States in 1914 to 1919. Stefano died in 1940 at the age of 30, possibly a war casualty.] From this east coast hotel, about 8 miles from the sea, we used to go swimming, getting there by bus or train, both fairly rickety. The swimming was good and the water surprisingly warm considering how far north we were. Swimming near the rocky headlands was, however, not to be recommended as this was the haunt of numerous small octopuses which the local fishermen caught in large numbers.

When the time came to set off back to Shanghai, Ian and the two girls set off separately as Ian and Mai-mai (Ross) were keen to have a few days golf in Japan. This did not greatly appeal to me so I set off to walk a couple of days over the mountains to where I could catch a train, stopping one night at a Korean 'inn' (in fact the hospice of a Buddhist monastery) beautifully clean and warm, although sleeping on tatami matting and supping on raw fish was a new experience. This two day walk was a great joy – lovely September weather with the leaves already taking on their autumn colours, particularly the maples which made brilliant splodges of red on the hillsides. Talking of red, many of the roofs in the Korean villages were a brilliant red from a distance, but this was in fact the chillies which had been harvested and put out to dry on the roofs of the peasants' houses.

From Keijo (Seoul) I had a very peaceful journey back to Nagasaki thanks to the good offices of a Japanese insurance man who saw me being subjected to the usual cross-examination by the Security men and intervened so effectively on my behalf that the whole of the rest of my journey went as smoothly as one could wish. This Japanese insurance man had spent some years in London and could not have been more helpful.

For Ian and the girls it was a very different story, as I found out when we met up again in Nagasaki. First of all, the fact that we had been a party of four on the outward journey and now there were only three of them raised the worst possible suspicions. On top of this, one of the hotels had supplied some wrong information and they had Ian down as a female and Mai-mai as a Mining Engineer from Australia – the fact that Mai-mai was wearing shorts may have encouraged this misapprehension! Both sides, having no common language and understanding each other very imperfectly, got very angry – Mai-mai refusing to answer questions because she was so upset that she did not dare to speak. All of this made the Japanese Police think that they were onto something big in the way of a spy-ring, and Ian and Mai-mai narrowly escaped being detained in Fusan. Thereafter their every movement was dogged, very obviously, until we all left Nagasaki – complete with our impounded books! I think that Ian and Mai-mai had their game of golf in Japan, but not in the relaxed atmosphere which they had anticipated.

[*Letter from Richard to his sister Maudie*]

c/o Sun Insurance Office,
1 The Bund
6 – 13 November 1938

My Dear Maudie,

About three weeks ago I started a letter to you which got as far as the third page, but it now seems so old that it has been torn up in disgust. By great good fortune I managed to get three weeks holiday in Korea in September and I got your letter when I came back. The trip to the Alps sounds grand; I must say I have a great weakness for that part of the world although I have only seen one small corner of it. I vaguely promised myself a visit there when I come home on leave [*which would not be until 1942*], but heaven knows what may have happened by then.

I don't know how you feel over this whole affair, [*the events leading up to the Munich Agreement and Neville Chamberlain's '…peace in our time…'*] probably rather differently to me because I am an out and out Chamberlainite. I think the only pity is that Chamberlain did not come into power about 10 years earlier with his policy of conciliation, because such a policy could have removed that feeling of humiliation (which admittedly has been very much exaggerated by Nazi propaganda) under which the Germans were living, and which was the chief reason that it was possible for a man like Hitler to attain the position he has done. Now Hitler is about the biggest menace in the world today. If the offer to revise the Treaty of Versailles (now admitted to have been a very poor treaty) had come from the Allied side we would be much better off than we are today. It is better to give a little with a magnanimous gesture than to let things slide until you are bullied into giving away a lot – which is what has happened.

Korea was a grand holiday – definitely the best I have had for many years; the holidays from London used to seem rushed and hectic and I did not come back feeling much better for them. Out here we do not officially get any local leave which is pretty short sighted because this is supposed to be a more trying climate than home and so one presumably needs a holiday more. I think the crux of the matter is probably that they are afraid the home staff will cut up rough because our 6 months home leave at the end of five years is more than they would get at home during those five years.

[*The next few pages of the letter describe in detail the journey from Shanghai to Fusan, that Richard has written about in the memoir.*]

From Fusan you have a full day's train journey up to Keijo, the capital of the country. The train was very crowded but by paying a few extra yen (1 yen = a halfpenny) we managed to get excellent seats in a First Class observation car at the tail end of the train, from which we got a grand view of the country which is well worth looking at. That night we stayed at the main hotel in Keijo – the first really comfortable night since leaving Shanghai.

The last lap of the journey is from Keijo to the Diamond Mountains, the last part of which is done in an electric train which goes through really grand scenery and for that reason is interesting all the way. The country is all mountainous and mostly very poor; the people look poor and their houses are all mud and wattle with thatched roofs. In some villages there are no solidly built buildings at all, the best being the school and the police station (both Japanese run) which are probably wood with a corrugated iron roof. In the larger townships these two buildings are often brick built, and there may also be a church, for strangely enough Christianity has more followers than any other religion in Korea, although the bulk of the population don't seem to worry too much about such matters.

The Korean language is different to Chinese and Japanese although all three use similar characters. Racially the Koreans are nearer the Chinese than the Japanese, although I believe there is a strong Mongolian element as there have been repeated Mongol invasions in the country's history. In dress too they are different both to the Japanese and the Chinese, for the women wear longish full skirts and blouses, more after the style of a European peasant woman. Korea was annexed by Japan sometime around the end of the last century and I believe there was a certain amount of unrest from time to time, but they seem to be settling down fairly well now although they are still apt to regard the Japanese as alien conquerors. As the younger Japanese-educated generation grows up I expect this feeling will gradually die out. The Japanese seem to be putting quite a lot of money into the country in the form of roads and railways and other development schemes, and the Koreans are probably much better off than they would be if still an independent state. The line from Fusan north is at present a single track affair, but it is being doubled, no doubt for military reasons as it carries on up to the Russian border eventually.

The Diamond Mountains are, mercifully, well off the beaten track and in a neighbourhood of no military importance; whilst we were there we were not troubled at all by the police and it seemed absolutely perfect after the rather artificial life one leads in Shanghai. The Diamond Mountains are on the eastern side of Korea, and the eastern side of the range is separated from the sea by a coastal plain only a few miles in width. There are two foreign (western) style hotels up there run by the Chosen (Korean) Government Railways, who are by way of developing the district as a holiday resort. Up to date, luckily from my own selfish point of view, they have not been overly successful. Although there are good paths everywhere in the mountains, one does not get the impression that the place is over popular or over populated.

On our way over from the west side of the mountains to the east, we stayed the night in a hut, modelled on an Alpine hut, where we made the acquaintance of a bloke from the Italian Embassy in Tokyo who struck me as being quite reasonable, but who did not go down so well with the ladies of the party (chiefly I think because of his continental mannerisms!). [*This was Count Stefano Macchi di Cellere.*]

Our news of the international crisis [*the events leading up to the Munich Agreement*] was very scanty and very stale (4 or 5 days old) and did not worry us very much until just at the end of the holiday when it caught us all in a very black mood. The others got rid of it by going to sleep after a heavy tiffin, and I by walking very quickly up a high mountain after the same – both methods probably equally effective according to our respective temperaments.

And now I had better stop; it is a month since I first started this letter and I want this to get to you by Christmas.

Anyway, all the best to you and Colin for Christmas and the New Year.

V. much love, Richard

Back in Shanghai I started playing Rugger again – the first time since some rather light-hearted efforts as a 'Trinity Trojan' [*Trinity College, Cambridge, rugby team*] some seven years before. Rugger in Shanghai was full of interest – principally because of the cosmopolitan nature of the city. Our opponents included the British Army garrison, sides from HM ships which happened to be in port, the American Marines, the French forces and the Japanese community. The British service teams played by the same rules that we did; the American Marines had to learn the difference in rules between American Football and Rugby Union and, to their credit, made a good shot of it. They took their Rugger very seriously and formed a Rugby Squad who went into special training and were put on a special diet; since they were selected for their physique and averaged a good 14 stone per man they would undoubtedly have wiped the floor with us if they had had longer to learn the game. The French played to more or less the same rules as us, but with their own Gallic interpretations; for instance, several of them wore berets on the field and, if a penalty of which they did not approve was given against them, it was not unknown for them to fling their berets at the ball as the penalty kick was about to be taken. I enjoyed playing against the Japanese as much as anyone because they knew the rules of the game and obeyed them meticulously; also they were a bit more my own size which was a nice change after contending with the American Marines. [*Richard stood 5 foot 5 inches and weighed around 9 stone!*]

Towards the end of the season in February 1939 I was lucky enough to be selected to represent Shanghai in the 'Inter-port' Rugby match against Hong Kong; this year it was an 'away' match which entailed a trip by sea in a Jardine's Coastal steamer, a week in Hong Kong (playing three matches) and a return by sea. On the way down to Hong Kong we called in at Swatow (a delightful place that had been one of the 'Treaty Ports'). The European houses were on an island across the harbour from the Chinese city – roomy colonial style mansions with high ceilings, wide verandahs and broad, sweeping lawns. Here, in order to keep ourselves fit, we played a light-hearted game of Soccer against a team from the small British destroyer which was in port at the time. The main match of the tour (against our opposite numbers, the Hong Kong Rugby Club) we managed to win, so we returned home well satisfied. My main recollections of Hong Kong are of beautiful weather (February, sunny and not too hot) and masses of flowers in the gardens of the houses in Kowloon. However the football pitches were bone hard; water supply on the island at that time of year was in those days a seasonal problem. My host for this delightful week in Hong Kong (which included a walk to the top of Tai Mo Shan, the highest point in the New Territories) was Claud Austin of the Phoenix Assurance who looked after the affairs of the 'Sun' in Canton and who, with many of the Hong Kong Volunteers, was to die in December 1941 in the fighting on Hong Kong Island.

On my return to Shanghai I was told that I was to be transferred to Singapore to take over supervision of the joint 'Sun/Liverpool, London & Globe/Thames & Mersey' Agency in that city where the existing incumbent had 'fallen apart'. So, after a fortnight of farewell parties culminating in a 'Black velvet' party with my charming Irish girlfriend of the day on board the P&O steamer RMS *RAWALPINDI* I set sail for Singapore at the beginning of March 1939. A mere matter of months later (in November 1939) the *RAWALPINDI*, by then an Armed Merchant Cruiser, was sunk in the North Atlantic after a brief but very gallant fight against impossible odds in the form of the German Battle Cruisers *SCHARNHORST* and *GNEISENAU*. Her Captain, Captain E.C. Kennedy RN, father of the well-known broadcaster Ludovic Kennedy, went down with his ship. [*Although many thought that he should have been awarded a Victoria Cross for this action, the only award he received was a posthumous Mention in Despatches. He is commemorated in the Chapel at Hampton Court Palace.*]

Chapter Two

Singapore and Penang 1939 to 1941

Within six months of Richard's arrival in Singapore, the Second World War had broken out but this initially had little impact in the Far East. Richard continued to work within the Sun office there until he was called up in June 1940 as the increasing belligerence of Japan started to be felt. It was also in June 1940, at a friend's wedding in Singapore, that he met Bobbie Couper Patrick, the girl who was to become his wife. He was commissioned into the Royal Army Service Corps, and posted to Penang Island, in north-west Malaya. This very pleasant posting included responsibility for RASC units throughout the northern part of the Malayan peninsula, and afforded him the opportunity to travel widely, on his motor cycle. Often this was on jungle roads that he identified in his reports as eminently suitable for lightly armed and mobile troops; to his chagrin, not being an officer from one of the 'fighting arms', his reports were not accorded great weight. Subsequent events were however to prove him right when the lightly equipped Japanese army used such roads to rapidly outflank British and Indian army fixed positions.

In December 1941 everything was to change. On 8 December 1941 Japanese carrier-borne aircraft, without warning, attacked the American Naval Base at Pearl Harbor in Hawaii. Simultaneously the Japanese Army landed at Kota Bharu in north east Malaya, and launched further attacks through southern Thailand into Perlis and Kedah in north-west Malaya. Two days later, on 10 December 1941, the battleship HMS **Prince of Wales** *and battlecruiser HMS* **Repulse** *under the command* *of Admiral Sir Tom Phillips were sunk by land-based Japanese bombers and torpedo bombers off the east coast of Malaya near Kuantan. They had been deployed from Singapore (without any effective air cover) to try to intercept the Japanese invasion convoy heading for Kota Bharu. By 12 December the speed of the Japanese advance resulted in a decision to evacuate Penang, and by 16 December Richard was back in Singapore.*

The successful evacuation of Penang was organised by a Royal Marines officer, Colonel Alan George Warren, CBE, DSC, a pre-war Fleet Air Arm pilot, who was serving in Military Intelligence at the outbreak of the European war. After Dunkirk he went to occupied France to look for any British army stragglers, escaping in a small boat to England. Sent to the Far East to command the Oriental Mission of the Special Operations Executive in early 1941, he later organised the evacuation of Penang, and after the fall of Singapore on 15 February 1942 he organised an escape route across Sumatra from the Indragiri River on the east coast to Padang on the west coast. Electing to stay behind to command the remaining British stragglers and casualties, he was taken prisoner by the Japanese. He kept his identity secret throughout three and a half years as a prisoner of war thus ensuring his survival. After the war he commanded 42 Commando Royal Marines, and left the service in 1953 to become a much-loved head of the English Department at Flint Hill, a private school in Oakton, Virginia, from 1957 to 1974. He died in 1975.

On his return to Singapore, Richard met up again with Bobbie Couper Patrick who had by then come down from Shanghai to work for the Ministry of Economic Warfare. The MEW was created in September 1939 on the outbreak of war with Germany to 'deprive the enemy of the material means of resistance and war making'. The Special Operations Executive was one of the functions of the MEW, being formed on 22 July 1940 under the Minister of Economic Warfare, Hugh Dalton. In practice, Bobbie was working for SOE, as she continued to do for the remainder of the war.

As the Japanese advance down the Malay peninsula accelerated, and the war-clouds gathered over Singapore, Richard and Bobbie became 'unofficially engaged' on Christmas Eve 1941. She was evacuated, along with all other SOE personnel, on 31 January 1942, two weeks before the fall of Singapore. The last large ships evacuating civilian and service personnel left Singapore on 11 February 1942. During the period 11 to 13 February several thousand women, children, civilian men and service personnel boarded the 46 ships (of all sizes, but mostly small) remaining in the harbour, bound for Fremantle (Australia) or Batavia (Java). Most were caught by Japanese bombers or naval forces as they threaded their way through the islands of the Riau and Lingga archipelagos and through the Banka Strait. Of the 46 ships that left Singapore, only 6 made it to safety. The death toll was very high, and most of the survivors spent the rest of the war in the privation and horrors of the Japanese internment camps in Sumatra, where death rates were up to thirty per cent. (This tragedy is well described in Geoffrey Brooke's book **Singapore's Dunkirk.***) Singapore surrendered to the Japanese on 15 February 1942.*

Returning again to Richard's memoir and letters, and a letter of Bobbie's describing her escape from Singapore…

Arrival in Singapore from 'never-a-dull-moment' Shanghai resulted in something of a shock to the system, as the job which I had come to take over had fallen apart in a big way. My predecessor (who was a Fellow of the Chartered Insurance Institute and infinitely better qualified than I in terms of insurance knowledge) had gone firmly on the bottle and let everything, job and family, slide. It was a depressing situation in which to take over, particularly as much of the work was completely new to me. Fortunately for the first 4 or 5 weeks I had the guidance of an Aussie, 'Cocky' Ballment, originally from the 'Sun' subsidiary in Java but promoted to a more senior post in Australia. He and the young Chartered Accountants from the firm of auditors who were sorting out the mess did a lot to restore my somewhat dented morale. I am still in touch with the CAs in question – Tom Cotterell and Eric ('Joe') Corless.

The first year after getting to Singapore was a fairly concentrated slog; long hours in the office, including weekends, with the only relaxation being a weekly game of Rugger on Saturday evening, an occasional game of squash and a weekly parade with the Singapore Royal Artillery (Volunteer), the SRA(V), affectionately known as 'The Battery'. This was part of the Singapore Volunteer Corps (SVC). When I had been in Singapore for almost exactly a year, I was able on Good Friday 1940 to sit down and write my final report to Head Office on the clearing up operation in the office. Thereafter I was able to devote more time to travelling up-country in Malaya, which I enjoyed a lot. I also became very air-minded for business travel (ahead of my time, I flatter myself), as I found I could catch an early morning flight to Kuala Lumpur or Ipoh, do a day's business, and catch the return flight to Singapore in the evening. This in effect saved me a full day by comparison with surface travel – an important consideration in a demanding one-man job. These flights were operated by Wearne's Air Services (an offshoot of one of the big garages in Singapore) flying De Havilland *Rapides*.

Life was also more relaxed because I had moved out of the Boarding House (quite a superior establishment called Manor House, in Chancery Lane) where I had lived for the first few months, to a very pleasant 'Bachelor Mess', No 1 Bishopsgate. This was an attractive colonial-style house with a garden and tennis court, situated in a very pleasant residential area of Singapore where beautiful mature trees were quite a feature. 'The Mess' was very efficiently run (without the efficiency being obtrusive) by the young Assistants from the firm of Chartered Accountants who had been so tolerant of my abysmal ignorance of accountancy when I first arrived in Singapore.

In the meanwhile, in September 1939, war had broken out in Europe, and in accordance with my obligations as a member of the Regular Army Reserve of Officers I reported to HQ Singapore Fortress at Fort Canning, and was informed that my services were not at the moment required. However, June 1940 saw two very important events in my life. First of all, after Dunkirk, the Army started 'scraping the bottom of the barrel' and I was informed that my services were indeed required. At the time however there was no OCTU (Officer Cadet Training Unit) in Malaya, so I was told that if I completed the two month 'embodiment' of the Volunteers with the Regular Forces (which was due to start at the end of the month) that would count as OCTU – providing I did not blot my copybook in the process. Head Office were accordingly informed by cable and arrangements were made for my place in the office to be taken by a member of the 'Royal'/'Liverpool, London & Globe' staff from Japan.

While all this was in train I had been asked by a former Shanghai insurance colleague, Sherwood Connor of the 'South British', to act as his Best Man at his wedding on 20 June 1940 to Betty Gordon, whom I had known in Shanghai and who, with her Bridesmaid, was coming down from Shanghai by sea. After various alarms and excursions, caused by the uncertain shipping schedules of that disturbed time, they arrived just one day before the wedding. And so, the second important event for me of that June 1940, I met officially the girl who so impressed me two and a half years before because she walked to work down Nanking Road, Shanghai, wearing a leopard skin coat! I approached this meeting with some trepidation because I had no idea whether we would be each other's 'cup of tea' for this rather important event. As it happened I could not have had an easier or more friendly greeting from Bobbie, sitting with the rest of the wedding party in a corner of the Singapore Cricket Club bar. Bobbie, at least outwardly, was completely at her ease despite the hassles of the journey and the fact that her Bridesmaid's dress had gone adrift somewhere. Fortunately a sampan trip out to the ship on which Bride and Bridesmaid had travelled, an elderly Butterfield and Swire steamer (the *NANCHANG*) lying out in The Roads, produced the missing dress (to my great relief, although Bobbie remarkably composed as ever had already worked out an alternative outfit for the wedding). That same afternoon she showed the same composure when, during a brief wedding rehearsal, Bobbie and I were lined up 'in loco' Bride and Groom (who were temporarily absent). The good lady who was organising the wedding and reception on behalf of the Groom remarked 'Now, you are the couple who ought to be getting married!' – we, who had only met three hours previously!

At the wedding itself Bobbie, who knew far more about the duties of a best man than I did, steered me charmingly and skilfully past the worst blunders which I might otherwise have made. From then on until the time came for Bobbie to return to Shanghai a fortnight later I found myself entertaining her on all possible occasions – the Bridesmaid whom I had originally thought that I, as Best Man, merely had a duty to look after on the day. So, it was dinner and dance at The Gap Restaurant or the Cathay, swimming at the Tanglin Club and tennis at The Mess at No1 Bishopsgate. There was one well remembered and happy evening when, my own car being 'in dock', Brinkmans (the firm of whose Insurance Department I was in charge) lent me a baby Mercedes – a cream coloured open two-seater with red trimmings and red upholstery. My first reaction was 'a real cad's car', but in fact, although not very high performance, it was a delightful car to drive and certainly the best I had driven up until then, and in its own generation as good as anything I have driven since. Bobbie was suitably impressed!

At the beginning of July, the SVC, of which I was a member, were called up for 'embodiment' with the Regular Forces. A few days later Bobbie sailed back to Shanghai in the Koninklijke Paketvaart-Maatschappij M.V. *TEGELBERG*, and I watched her sail out through The Heads with very mixed feelings, as I wondered what Bobbie was going back to. My viewpoint was the lawn of the Royal

Singapore Yacht Club whose hallowed turf we brutal and licentious soldiery were digging up to make a gun position for our 18 pounder guns; this fact alone was indicative that there was at the time quite a 'flap' on – hence my unease at Bobbie going back to Shanghai. Fortunately the 'flap' did not at that time mature, but the Japanese were making some very rude noises, as well they might with the whole of Europe in German hands and Britain standing completely on her own. Despite this, there was a curious feeling of exhilaration in the air which, according to friends returning to Singapore from Home Leave, also prevailed in the UK.

The *TEGELBERG* was a very fine-looking 14,000 ton motor vessel with handsome lines – a fine sight as she sailed through The Heads in her war-time grey paint. This was only a matter of 6 or 7 weeks after Holland had been over-run by the Germans, and the Dutch members of the ship's company found themselves in an unenviable position as their country was under German occupation and they probably had no news of what might have happened to their families. In the case of the ship's Doctor, whom Bobbie got to know, his fiancée lived in Rotterdam, which was heavily bombed in the first days of the invasion, and he still had no news of her.

The 'embodiment' in the SRA(V) ('The Battery') I thoroughly enjoyed on account of the fairly strenuous open-air life, the happy atmosphere in 'The Battery' and the good relationship, anyway at NCO level, with the Regular Gunners to whose Corporals' Mess we had free access (I by that time having been promoted to the dizzy heights of Bombardier – a fine sounding rank and one of the best in the British Army).

After two months 'embodiment' I was duly commissioned into the RASC [*Royal Army Service Corps*]. That was not my choice as I naturally wanted to go into a Gunner unit but, as it turned out, it was a very good thing because the locally commissioned Gunners were all posted to Coast Defence where they never fired a shot in anger, whereas in Penang (whither I was shortly transferred) I was involved in Supply and Motor Transport for the whole of Northern

Malaya. Here I was able to see far more of the country than I would have done in my civilian job and infinitely more than I would have done sitting on my backside in a concrete gun emplacement. The posting to Penang, which came about within a matter of a few weeks, was, as I have always understood, a punishment for a minor breach of discipline (late on parade on a Sunday morning after a rather hectic Saturday night out). Penang, militarily, was considered to be a complete 'dead end' – 'You'll get no promotion this side of the ocean' in the words of the army ballad. This did not worry me (an Emergency Soldier) as I had visited Penang on business in civilian life and had been greatly taken by the place. Anyway, the posting to Penang was one of the best punishments I have ever had and one which I have never regretted.

[*Letter from Richard to his sister Maudie*]

R.A.S.C. Malaya
11 January 1941

My Dear Maudie

All of my letters to you seem to start off with a very necessary apology for not having written for a very long time (and yours to me ditto), but I'm afraid the apology is far more necessary from my side. I have found amongst my unanswered correspondence one letter from you written to me in Shanghai, but I can't believe that I have been as lax as all that.

Except for the first two months I was in the Army in Singapore, life has been very busy indeed for a long time past. It took me a full year to get the old job in Singapore properly cleared up; the anniversary of my arrival in Singapore was Good Friday and I celebrated it by spending the whole day in the office writing a long report on my activities during that year. Actually I was quite pleased with myself, as I was paying all expenses and losses and after that remitting $10,000 (over £1,000) home every quarter, and building up a biggish reserve out here to meet emergencies.

Even after that I always had plenty to do but I could get through my work in an 8-hour day and had my weekends free.

April and May were both busy as I did a good deal of travelling in order to rake up more business. June I was told that I was going to be called up. It was also a rather fierce month as I had a week's visit from a bloke from Shanghai, and after that a wedding (also a Shanghai connection) at which I was Best Man. July the War Office had still not confirmed my commission, so I was 'embodied' with the Volunteer Gunners (Singapore Volunteer Corps Artillery) for continuous training. They put us through it good and proper, but I thoroughly enjoyed myself as Bombardier Laird; I am convinced that Bombardier (or Corporal) is the best rank possible for a 'do' like that. The only snag was that I had to go into the office every afternoon and do a few hours intensive brain-work which did not suit me very well. Also having been up since 6 o'clock working in the sun all morning one really needed a bit of rest, as we went on parade again at 5 o'clock and also had the odd night shoots to do. I was a bit weary by the end of the first month, but slept the clock round once and felt fitter than I had done since I first got to Singapore. We had a break of 10 days, during which I had to get the office straight and finish my Head Office Accounts for the 2nd Quarter. My relief arrived from Shanghai on 5th August and to my great gratification I managed to have everything up to date for him the previous evening. A couple of days later I went back to do the second spell of Volunteer training which was even better than the first; I still had to go into the office every day, but the show was very much more efficiently run and they relaxed some of the petty points of Regular Army discipline.

   I was commissioned as soon as the Volunteer training was finished (September 1940) and was put onto the MT side of the RASC to start with. I was fairly busy at first but we got several new officers at the end of September and the work had to be split up. In the middle of November I was sent up here to Penang – temporarily at first but it was made permanent as another bloke was seconded to the RAF and I took his place. I was not really sorry to leave Singapore as I never really liked the place and I certainly did not get nearly so dug in there as I did in Shanghai. It was a pity having to leave the house where I was living as it was certainly a delightful spot, but

I would have had to have gone from there eventually to the new RASC Officers Mess.

I did see the Bells once before I left Singapore, but they were very hard to get at, living out at the Naval Base. [*The Naval Base was at Sembawang, on the north side of Singapore Island. Captain Frederick Secker Bell CB ('Hookie') and his Australian wife, Dulcie, were friends of Colin and Maudie Gatey. 'Hookie' Bell had commanded the cruiser HMS* Exeter *at the Battle of the River Plate in December 1939, in which three British cruisers had engaged the German pocket battleship* Graf Spee, *an action that resulted in her being scuttled off Montevideo a few days later. In 1941 he was serving as Chief Staff Officer to Commodore, Malaya.*] Also I found it a bit difficult to find a suitable way of entertaining them – I, a bachelor and a very junior Army subaltern, and he a senior and very distinguished Captain Royal Navy. I really would have liked to have seen more of them and I should have felt a good deal better able to cope with the situation if I had still been in 'civvy' life.

Penang is a pleasant restful spot after Singapore where latterly I knew far too many people for the good of my health. It's a place where one makes a lot of acquaintances, but very few real friends (rather a prevalent complaint all over the Far East).

Shanghai seems to be pretty grim nowadays; almost all my friends from there have packed up their jobs and volunteered in a bunch. I saw them all in Singapore at the beginning of October on their way through to join an OCTU. The young women seem to be getting married in a rush – many of them rather in desperation as far as I can judge. I heard today that many firms are offering to pay wives' and families' passages away from the place, indicating that they may not be prepared to do so later on.

So far as I am concerned, I look like being here indefinitely as things are expanding so rapidly that they are not likely to send anyone away home – unfortunately. At the moment I am doing a captain's job and, although I have been recommended for the acting rank, I don't think I am likely to get it as I am so very junior.

As far as I can gather the Japs are behind the Thais at the moment and at the same time they have troops in parts of Indo-China; all very tricky. They are definitely out to get themselves established within striking distance of Malaya, but I don't think they are likely to move against us just yet, unless things get very black at home.

I am sending this c/o Henri [*his brother Henry*] as I don't know whether you will still be at the old place.

V. much love to you, and all the best to both of you for 1941,
Richard

On arrival at Penang I was stationed at Glugor Cantonment where my job was adjutant to OC RASC [*Officer Commanding Royal Army Service Corps*], who was responsible for Supply and Transport arrangements for Penang Island, Northern Perak and the whole of Kedah and Perlis. My CO was a regular officer from the RIASC (Royal Indian Army Service Corps) who was a very broad-minded individual (having, inter alia, spent over 2 years in Peking learning Mandarin, which he spoke fluently). As a result, as long as I got on with the job, I had a free hand to travel extensively in Northern Malaya – something very few regimental Officers would have been able to do.

I was at that time a keen hill-walker and motor-cyclist (in that order), not interests which normally go together, but the combination of these interests enabled me to see, with great enjoyment, as much of Northern Malaya as a brief 15 months allowed. My walking was confined to the hills of Penang Island and Kedah Peak on the mainland. This included a walk from the top station of the Penang Hill Railway across the hills for a bathe in a delectable waterfall above the main road at the north-west corner of the island. Later I was warned off this practice as the waterfall was said to be infested with a bug which penetrated the soles of the feet and caused various problems; fortunately I got the warning before any damage was done. I also walked out to the lighthouse and Signal Station at Muka Head. The lighthouse is normally supplied by launch, but there was a roughish path along the coast used by the engineers maintaining the telephone line to the lighthouse; at the foot of the headland on which the lighthouse is built there was an idyllic sandy beach where one could bathe after struggling along the rough path. On these walks there was a surprising amount of wildlife to be seen; a wide variety of birds (about which at that time I unfortunately did not know very much), iguanas and troops of monkeys in the Forest Reserve and, on the coast, otters. The Penang skyline is dominated by Kedah Peak on the mainland (about 4,000 feet high) to which, as a keen hill-walker, I was immediately attracted. I went up twice; once on foot and once on my motorcycle. On foot I was followed down the mountain by a pack of wild, or semi-wild, dogs; an alarming experience and I was not sorry when they made off after other game.

[*In February 1941, Richard and Maudie's elder brother Henry was killed in an accident in the blackout. He was a Home Guard motorcycle despatch rider.*]

[*Letter from Richard to his sister Maudie*]

Glugor Cantonment,
Penang
29 March 1941

My Dear Maudie

It was only yesterday that I got Barbie's cable about Henry's death, so God knows what she thinks of me as a brother-in-law and head of the family. The cable got to Singapore on 7th March, but they have recently established an Army Post Office in Malaya (to improve the efficiency of the postal service!) and that is what happens. Don't I love some of those b------s in Singapore.

The news really did come as an awful shock, although I suppose one must be prepared for anything these days. The trouble is that you are never quite ready for anything when it is really close and personal. As yet I have no details of his death, but I'd be willing to bet that directly or indirectly it was something to do with this wretched war.

My real object in writing this is to ask about Barbie and to find out how much there is left for her; I may be wrong, but I rather fancy not an awful lot. I have not said anything to Barbie herself about helping her out, because I am afraid she would be much too proud to accept anything, but I do consider that I above everyone am the right and natural person to do anything that is needed – and I want to do it. [*Richard instructed his bank in England to make Barbie an annual allowance of £100 (around £5,000 in 2019 terms).*] It might be necessary to change any arrangements that may be made if I were to get married myself, but there is no immediate prospect of that and anyway we can make alterations later if I do get married.

I have put this proposition up to Laces [*the Laird family solicitors*] and I am writing to you also because I think you have more influence with Barbie than the rest of the family, and I hope they will not have their noses put out of joint because I am writing to you. The real people to fix the thing, if necessary, are Laces, but I would be really glad if you could use your influence in the right direction with the Elephant. [*Barbie's family nickname was 'Jumbo', for reasons unknown (she was quite slight).*]

I am now a Captain (Acting, but paid) but life gets busier and busier and looks like going on that way; however it is satisfactory to be able to feel you are doing a proper job of work at last.

I am sending this c/o Laces as I imagine you will very likely have left Rochester by now.

Good-bye for the time being, with v. much love, Richard

With my arrival in Penang I had to my joy escaped from a rather hum-drum civilian office routine and had little real need for a car; fortunately a little-used 350 cc Ariel 'Red Hunter' motorcycle more or less fell into my lap at a very modest price. With the 'Red Hunter' I was able to get around extensively on the mainland visiting various military units and installations, and was also able to do one or two reconnaissances along tracks not normally used by motor vehicles. One such was from Kelian Intan down to Grik which was perfectly passable for a jeep or motorcycle and on which I reported at the time. It was also obviously well known to the Japanese as subsequent events were to prove, although one heard later that our people had been 'caught by surprise' when the Japanese out-flanked them by coming down that Grik road. Another 'reccy' ended in a minor disaster when I followed a road trace through secondary jungle where numerous creeks were bridged by unguarded narrow wooden plank bridges. At what turned out to be the very last such bridge, being by then tired after a long hot morning in the Malayan sun, I finished up in the creek with my long-suffering 'Red Hunter' (which, alas, was later to find its last resting place in a watery grave). Fortunately, the first person to come along was an extremely helpful Malay District Officer who quickly organised a gang of coolies to fish the bike out of the creek and ship it down to Penang, where it was quickly and efficiently returned to full strength and vigour by the Chinese Agents for Ariel, from whom I had bought the bike.

One of my most vivid recollections of my time in Penang was the enjoyable duty of going down to a small pier near the Cantonment at Glugor to collect Confidential mail off the 'C' Class Empire Flying Boats which touched down there en route from Rangoon to Singapore. These flying boats were, to my way of thinking, one of the most beautiful aircraft I have ever seen; a lasting memory is of these aircraft touching down with a flash of brilliant white spray on the bright blue water, against a background of the dark green wooded hills of the mainland.

Penang produced another notable experience for me in that for the first and only time I piloted an aircraft, namely a Short *Singapore* Flying Boat. This had four engines, two 'pusher' and two 'puller', a maximum speed of 100 knots and was one of the noisiest aircraft that ever was. A flight of them was stationed at Penang from time to time with the aircrews living in the Mess at Glugor, where one of the pilots gave me the chance of taking over the controls on a test flight. The *Singapores*' job at Penang was to fly patrols out into the Indian Ocean looking for German Armed Raiders. This was a task which the aircrews, with good reason, did not relish as the Raiders carried a very heavy armament, including anti-aircraft guns, and the old, slow *Singapores* would have been sitting ducks. Fortunately no aircraft were lost to the Raiders and the *Singapores* were withdrawn and replaced by *Catalinas*. I have never heard how many of them survived, but I did hear that some of the *Catalinas* finished up at Soerabaya in Java, where elements of the Dutch Army, infected by the quislingitis of some of the occupied countries of Europe, refused to let them take off. (By all accounts this malaise did not affect the Dutch Navy or Air Force.)

With all my other activities I had little time, and not much inclination, for social life, but I do remember visiting both the E & O and Runnymede Hotels. Both were beautifully situated by the sea, and both had in common a hemi-spherical dome over the dance floor which acted like a sounding board so that one could clearly hear the conversation going on at the table diametrically opposite – entertaining or embarrassing according to one's point of view! There was a similar hemi-spherical dome over the dance floor at the Sea View Hotel in Singapore.

On the outbreak of the Japanese War at the beginning of December 1941 all combatant troops except the men manning the two Coast Defence Batteries moved over to the mainland leaving only base units on the island. After some days of Japanese bombing (of Georgetown and the harbour rather than military installations) the evacuation of Penang Island (military personnel and European civilians) was ordered following the Japanese breakthrough at Jitra [*in northern Kedah, about 120 kilometres north of Penang, on 11/12 December 1941*]. Militarily Penang Island was not defensible with the troops available on the island, and the evacuation order caused much distress among the European Government Servants who were devoted to Penang and its people. Military vehicles and stores were destroyed as far as possible in the time available, and with the personnel available. Having dealt with my official responsibilities I personally pushed my car over the quay at Penang Harbour Board where, in happier days, P&O, Blue Funnel and Glen and Shire liners had tied up. At the last minute I was able to arrange to put my beloved 'Red Hunter' on one of the two Penang ferries (*TANJONG* and *BAGAN*, if I remember rightly) which were being used for the evacuation, whilst I joined my RASC detachment on the other ferry. We lay down on the steel car deck pretty well all in and went to sleep, only to be woken up some hours later by the sound of gunfire and to find that we had not even left Penang Harbour. All of this caused considerable alarm and despondency, as we feared that the Nips [*Japanese*] had got amongst us.

The explanation was, however, that as a result of the bombing the Malay crews of the ferries had, not unnaturally, deserted, and scratch crews from the *PRINCE OF WALES* and *REPULSE* (sunk a mere 48 hours previously) had been sent up from Singapore to Penang to man the ferries. Not being familiar with the engines they had not been able to raise sufficient steam on the ferry carrying my 'Red Hunter'. The personnel on board that ferry had been transferred to other ships and the ferry had been sunk by gunfire – hence my reference earlier to a watery gave for my 'Red Hunter'. By first light we were still well within sight of Penang Island as the surviving ferry had been making very slow progress; all except a skeleton crew were therefore transferred to the Straits Steamship *PANGKOR* which had been taken over by the RNVR [*Royal Naval Volunteer Reserve*] and was flying the White Ensign. If the Nips had found us we should have been a 'sitting duck', but fortunately they did not (although we felt decidedly naked until after nightfall). I spent the rest of the day on the Boat Deck of the ship with men of my unit acting as a Lewis Gun and rifle anti-aircraft (!) Section. Not much hope if the Nips had found us, but at least we could have made a gesture of fighting back, and it was better than being battened down below decks. In due course (about 36 hours) we arrived at Singapore without, marvellous to relate, any incidents. It is also pleasing to relate that the surviving Penang Ferry and her skeleton crew in due course arrived safely at Port Swettenham.

As a postscript to the evacuation of Penang it is interesting to record that on the military (as opposed to the civilian) side this operation was organised by a Colonel Warren, Royal Marines,

Singapore and Penang 1939 to 1941   51

who had been sent up from Singapore specially for the purpose. Colonel Warren was a first class bloke to work under, or more accurately with, as he was very easy to get on with. I was very flattered to learn subsequently that in his report on this operation he had made some complimentary remarks about my efforts in Penang, the more so since the end of the story is typical of the man. From later history of the events of this time I have learnt that Colonel Warren was in fact a member of Special Operations Executive, and was responsible for organising the escape route across Sumatra to Padang on the west coast, whence considerable numbers of Service personnel [*and a small number of civilians*] got away to India/Ceylon and Australia. He himself refused to leave until he was satisfied that all available shipping and local craft had got away. Having remained until the last he was captured by the Japanese and was reported to have died quite early on in one of the Sumatra POW camps, where conditions were notoriously bad.

PS to the previous paragraph.

However it seems from a recent (1985) account of SOE operations in Malaya ('SOE Singapore 1941/1942' by Richard Gough) that Colonel Warren did survive the war, having been sent up to Thailand with one of the early working parties on 'The Railway' [*the Burma-Siam Railway, of which more later*]. It is possible that the report of him having died in one of the Sumatra camps was put about deliberately to throw the Nips off the scent, since obviously they would dearly have loved to get hold of Colonel Warren of SOE Malaya.

PPS to previous paragraph.

Among those whom Colonel Warren ordered to sail from Padang in a commandeered junk were Ivan Lyon [*Lieutenant Colonel Ivan Lyon, MBE, DSO, Gordon Highlanders*] and Jock Campbell [*A successful planter in Malaya – later Major, OBE*] (who come into the story later on). Others who made a successful escape included Davis [*John Davis – Police, later Lieutenant Colonel,*

CBE, DSO] and Broome [*Richard Broome – a senior civil servant, later Colonel, OBE, MC*] who later in the war went back into Malaya by submarine for Force 136 [*the Far East arm of SOE*]. After some delay they managed to join up with Spencer Chapman ('The Jungle is Neutral') [*Lieutenant Colonel Freddie Spencer Chapman, DSO and Bar*] and went on to play a distinguished part in organising guerrilla resistance to the Japanese.

[*All of those named above (Warren, Lyon, Campbell, Davis, Broome and Spencer Chapman) were founding members of the 'Oriental Mission' formed in January 1941 to conduct SOE operations in the Far East, under the command of Colonel Warren. This eventually became part of Force 136, the SOE Mission in India.*]

During the time I had been in Penang I had corresponded intermittently with Bobbie back in Shanghai and, shortly before I left Penang, I received a letter from her saying she was leaving Shanghai to take up a job in Singapore (with the Ministry of Economic Warfare as it later turned out), and that she would be staying with Betty Connor at a house in Barker Road off the Bukit Timah Road. [*Betty Connor was the girl at whose wedding to Sherwood Connor she and Richard had met in June 1940 as bridesmaid and best man*]

As a newly arrived evacuee from Penang the Army did not know what to do with me, but that very evening I was able to scrounge some transport (how I missed my 'Red Hunter') and go out to Barker Road where Bobbie, standing at the top of the steps of the bungalow and looking more attractive than ever, greeted me with every indication of genuine pleasure – what had I been doing in the 18 months since I had last seen her?! Betty Connor, who was expecting a baby, was very wisely leaving for Australia very shortly but Bobbie was staying in the house 'pro tem' so, by mutual consent, I fixed to go and see her as often as possible. For this purpose I was determined not to be dependent on being able to scrounge transport, so I bought myself a push-bike which became my means of transport for my courtship – not very conventional for a European in Singapore in those days, but it served my purpose very well.

After getting back from Penang I reported to Singapore Fortress, who obviously did not know what on earth to do with me. For three or four weeks I found myself arranging passages for women and children who were being evacuated, as the writing was obviously on the wall for a sticky time ahead. After my active and energetic life in Northern Malaya and the excitement of getting away from Penang I found this job extremely frustrating. The only consolation was that Bobbie was around and during those three or four weeks I was able to see her fairly regularly (thanks to the push-bike!) at the house in Barker Road where she was on her own, and later at a Boarding House in Oxley Road, to which she had wisely moved. We celebrated Christmas Eve (1941) at the house in Barker Road, whither I went armed with a bottle of champagne and, as a Christmas present, a small string of cultured pearls. Years afterwards I heard of the superstition that pearls betoken tears; in view of the events of the next few years perhaps the superstition had something in it. Nevertheless, we finished that evening pledged to each other to get married 'when the war is over'; the pledge was duly redeemed but not until a good deal of water had flowed under the bridges for both of us.

Those few evenings at Barker Road always seemed marvellously peaceful and I have no recollections of being disturbed by air raid alarms. One lovely Malayan night Bobbie walked a little of the way home with me along Balmoral Road, a beautiful tree-lined road. So peaceful did it seem that I, very wrongly as I now feel, allowed her to walk back to the house on her own, but 'le bon dieu' must have been watching over us, as indeed he continued to do in the years to come, and she arrived home without incident. We came to know Balmoral Road quite well in the years after the war when we were living nearby in Ewe Boon Road and still remember it with affection. [*After they were married in London in January 1946, they had returned to Singapore.*]

About the middle of January 1942 I was, to my great relief, taken off my frustrating desk job in Singapore and sent up-country to join 'West Force', a joint British/AIF [*Australian Imperial Force – the name given to Australian army personnel who had volunteered to serve outside Australia*] organisation which had been hastily set up to establish Supply and Transport services in Southern Malaya, which were virtually non-existent owing to the rapid advance of the Japanese down the Malayan peninsula. The furthest north I got was to a small Supply Depot about 6 miles north of Segamat in Northern Johore. It was a rather eerie atmosphere in this Supply Depot as it was manned by an RIASC section composed entirely of Indian personnel who, but for my presence, were all ready to bolt for it. At night it was particularly 'nervy' as we could hear gunfire up ahead not so far away, and there was a constant stream of vehicles withdrawing down the main road. I consoled myself by writing the odd letter to Bobbie which, happy to relate, did get through. In the evenings at dusk two or three Vickers *Wildebeests* (old biplanes with a maximum speed of 120 knots originally designed to carry torpedoes) would fly over not much above tree-top height to bomb Japanese vehicles and troop concentrations. These were real suicide missions and I had infinite admiration for the men flying those 'planes – all that we had, a measure of our nakedness.

I think we managed to keep supplies going to the troops in our area (those who in those confused times knew where to find us) but I, and even more so my Indian Supply Section, were not sorry when the order came to clear out. Even so, when we went over the river bridge at Segamat the REs [*Royal Engineers*] were just about ready to blow it. Segamat itself was like a ghost town; shops all boarded up and the only people on the streets a few furtive looters. From now on it was retreat all the way. At Genuang Station 5 or 6 miles south of Segamat a train had been bombed and, although the track had not been badly damaged, there were no facilities for repairing it. Included in the train's load were two truck loads of freshly baked bread from the Singapore Cold Storage (something

British units were crying out for). I informed any British unit I was able to contact but, such was the speed of the retreat, I doubt if any were able to collect much of the bread.

The main cross-roads at Ayer Hitan on the north/south trunk road was a shambles following a recent Japanese air attack. Further south on the road to Pontian Kecil in the south-west corner of Johore there was a sizeable Supply depot in a former rubber factory, but it had no telephone communication (probably owing to the telephone lines having been cut by fifth columnists). I therefore had the job of going out on a motor-cycle to bring in the personnel manning the Depot. It was a beautiful moonlit night, but a rather eerie experience as no-one knew where the Nips were and there were odd rifle shots going off in the rubber plantations through which the road ran. However, I got there without incident and was relieved to find the Supply section all loaded up and ready to leave.

The following morning, 30 January 1942, we crossed the Causeway onto Singapore Island and found a temporary bivouac in the rubber on Bukit Sembawang Estate, a mile or so from the end of the Causeway. Across the road from our bivouac were a charming Chinese family who spoke good English and were most helpful in allowing us to draw water from their supply. Even at that time I wondered how they would fare once the Japanese tried to land on the Island and, in view of what happened so shortly afterwards, I have often wondered even more what became of them.

By now my job on the Mainland (Adjutant to OC RASC West Force – the short-lived organisation formed to try and hold the Japanese in northern Johore) had folded up, and my CO gave me permission to go into the City of Singapore. I made use of these few hours of leave to ring up Bobbie's office (Ministry of Economic Warfare in the Cathay Building) to see if she was still there. She was not only there, but to my great surprise and pleasure her boss (Mr Miskin, who had been with the APC [*Asiatic Petroleum Company*] in Shanghai and looked with favour on Bobbie because of her Shanghai background, and other sterling qualities) gave her permission to come down-town and meet me. This we did at the Singapore Cricket Club, and sat and talked at the very same table in the Bar where, on 19 June 1940, we had first met on the day before Sherwood Connor and Betty Gordon were married. It was here that Bobbie gave me a Chinese Silver Dollar (an impressive coin) as a good luck talisman. Subsequently we went along to Gammeters (Swiss Watch Shop) on Collyer Quay as I needed to replace my wrist-watch which, what with long hours of driving trucks and lorries and riding motor cycles, had disintegrated. Both the Silver Dollar and the wrist-watch from Gammeters come into the story later. So, on Collyer Quay, we said goodbye to each other with, for my part, so much to say but so much left unsaid. We knew very little of what the future would hold for us except that I thought that there would be one hell of a battle for Singapore which would involve ALL troops, including RASC personnel in actual fighting. Little did I know that the whole thing would disintegrate in a little over two weeks.

At that time MEW were due to move to Batavia in Java at short notice, which I did not feel would be any more healthy than Singapore, as by that time (end of January 1942) the Nips were already established in Dutch Borneo and the Celebes. I therefore urged Bobbie to move on to Australia if she had any choice in the matter, as she did have relatives there.

That evening (30 January) having again been told that I was not needed 'pro tem', I went to Bobbie's boarding house in Oxley Rise hoping to say to her some of the things which I had not got around to that afternoon, but was told by the 'Boy' who had been looking after her that 'Missy sudah pengi' [*literally, 'Missy completely departed'*]; sadly no clues as to where she might be. So I went to the house in Cable Road where George and Maisie Keyzar lived (George having been my Section Commander in 'The Battery' [*Singapore Royal Artillery (Volunteer)*]) and was lucky to find them both there. George had been given leave as Maisie (newly out of hospital with a week-old baby, plus a boy aged 2 years old) was due to leave for UK via South Africa next day in the *DUCHESS OF BEDFORD*. She arrived, happily, in UK in due course after a not very comfortable voyage. I have a vivid memory of sitting in the peace and quiet of the Keyzars' lamp-lit sitting room drinking a stengah (or stengahs!) [*whisky and soda with ice*] and wondering what was to become of all of us; Bobbie included as it was only a matter of six hours since I had said goodbye to her, and the Keyzars did know her from the wedding junketings in June 1940. Fortunately all of us survived, and were able to renew and expand on a real and lasting friendship after the war – not one of the passing acquaintances which are so easy to form and then lose track of. [*I remember the Keyzars well. Sadly George died shortly after my father wrote his memoir in 1987.*]

Since Bobbie sailed for Java on 31 January 1942 my CO, Major R.W. Dobson ('Dobbie'), had been given a new job as OC Base Supply Depot, Singapore; I continued as his Adjutant. Base Supply Depot (BSD) always seemed a rather grandiose title, considering that the area which we supplied was confined to Singapore Island (and even that did not last for very long!) and there were only a handful of outlying depots to be looked after. BSD itself consisted of two or three Singapore Harbour Board (SHB) godowns [*warehouses*] adjoining SHB Gate No.8. In the brief spell between the blowing of the Causeway at the end of January and the Japanese landing on the Island on 8 February an unnatural lull descended, broken by Japanese air raids in which, encouragingly, our Anti-Aircraft batteries did score some successes. During this period we returned each evening to a commandeered house in Thomson Road near the junction with Chancery Lane; this I remember as an oasis of peace and quiet where I started reading (but never finished owing to being overtaken by more urgent matters) a book found in the house – *The Sun is my Undoing*.

It was during the first week in February 1942 that I called in at my old civilian Mess (No.1 Bishopsgate) where I found a curiously peacetime atmosphere. Most of the members of the Mess assembled to drink to the future now that Singapore was indeed an Island, the Causeway having been blown two or three days previously. The Chinese 'Boys' were serving drinks just as in the old days. But my outstanding memory of that occasion was of a very attractive girl called Peggy Green, wife of a young Singapore lawyer, Bobbie Green. Among much talk of evacuation of women and children this girl who was, I think, doing VAD (Voluntary Aid Detachment) work, was most emphatic that nothing, repeat nothing, would persuade her to join 'rats leaving the sinking ship' and, as I always thought of her as a girl of character, I am sure she meant it. I heard later that she had been lost in the disastrous last-minute evacuation of Singapore on Friday 13 February 1942; she was last seen in the water badly wounded after the sinking of one of the evacuation ships, but steadfastly refused all help. I often wondered how she came to be on one of the evacuation ships, but can only think that she must have been given a direct order to leave. [*In fact, Peggy Green, although wounded, did survive the sinking of the ship in which she was travelling, but did not live through internment in one of the women's camps in Sumatra, where conditions were notoriously harsh.*] Bobbie Green survived as a POW in Thailand, and even had their dachshund dog with him who also survived right through the war; unfortunately I never heard the full story which, knowing POW life, must have been a remarkable one. [*This is not the only such story.* The Judy Story *by E. Varley tells of an English Pointer, Judy, who survived the sinking of the ship on which she escaped from Singapore and 3½ years in Sumatra prison camps, and was subsequently awarded the Dickin Medal (the PDSA 'Animal VC') in 1946 on her return to England.*]

On the night of 7/8 February all hell let loose in the form of a very heavy artillery barrage and in the morning the news came through that the Japanese had succeeded in crossing the Straits of Johore and landing on the north-west coast of the Island. As the house in Thomson Road was needed for troops stationed in that part of the Island we moved down to the SHB godowns where the BSD was situated.

Of the week that followed I only remember odd incidents. For instance, the outlying Supply Depot in the rubber plantations down a track off the far end of Thomson Road manned by an elderly RIASC officer with an Indian section, but with no telephone about which he was justifiably nervous. When the extent and speed of the Japanese advance became clear I went out to try and get this Section in, but too late as they had already been overrun by the Japanese. The RIASC officer was not one to leave his post until ordered and did not survive; one felt sad and upset as a telephone could well have saved him. Going out to another Supply Depot at Nee Soon we found a scene of panic and confusion; the only stable element in this depressing scenario was a Gurkha unit withdrawing through the rubber, section covering section, all in perfect order.

On Wednesday 11 February, after a heavy Japanese air raid on the SHB area, I walked down to the wharf to see what damage had been done. There I found the French ship *FELIX ROUSSEL* (Messageries Maritime – easily recognisable by her square funnels); she was undamaged but completely deserted although the 'All Clear' had gone some five or ten minutes before. I went on board (no guard on the gangway) and walked all round the upper deck without seeing a soul; a ghost ship and a most eerie experience. In the next berth was the *EMPIRE STAR* (Blue Star Line) but she was still manned. Both ships did get away that night or the next morning and did get clear away, although the *EMPIRE STAR* did suffer some serious bomb damage on the passage down to Java. These were the last ships of any size to get away from Singapore before the disastrous evacuation attempt on the notorious and unlucky Friday 13 February 1942. It was on Tuesday 10 February that General Wavell (who at the turn of the year had been appointed Commander-in-Chief ABDA (American, British, Dutch and

Australian Forces)) issued his Special Order of the Day which included the following passages:

> Commanders and Senior Officers must lead their men and if necessary die with them: there must be no thought or question of surrender: every unit must fight it out to the end and in close contact with the enemy.
>
> I look to you and your men to fight to the end and to prove that the fighting spirit that won the Empire still exists to defend it.

Some of us were naive enough to take that Special Order of the Day seriously, so that events of a mere five days later (when Singapore surrendered) left one feeling that so many of the things one believed in had been given up without a real fight.

Impressions of those remaining five days before Singapore surrendered are made up of isolated incidents. After General Wavell's Special Order of the Day many of us in the RASC expected to be formed into Infantry Companies in order to at least give what support we could to the front-line troops, but as far as I know no move was ever made to do this – so much for Wavell's last man, last round order. I know of one RASC MT (Motor Transport) Company officer who shot himself in disgust when the surrender order did come. There were the usual air raids on the Harbour Board area, but only small anti-personnel bombs were dropped in the area of the BSD godowns; they caused no casualties as all personnel had been trained to use slit trenches which were adequate in number and depth.

Driving into Singapore one afternoon I met AS, my CO from Penang days, who had his wife with him; she was a trained Nursing Sister and was now working at the Singapore General Hospital. Both of them seemed to be in good form and remarkably cheerful, which rather surprised me at this late stage in the 'piece'. AS had told me in Penang days that he would never let his wife fall into the hands of the Japanese alive, and that they had a suicide pact to ensure this did not happen. It therefore came as no surprise to me to learn later that when Singapore surrendered they put their pact into practice, but apparently got the dosage of their potion wrong with the result that AS survived but his wife died. A sad business as they had both been extremely kind to me in Penang.

On either the Friday or Saturday before Singapore surrendered (13 or 14 February) another officer and myself were detailed to go to the Medical Comforts Store near Alexandra Hospital and, armed with axes, to destroy all the alcohol held there (Brandy, Champagne, Rum, Whisky etc) in case it should fall into the hands of the Nips and cause them to go berserk (which it no doubt would have done). In the light of later knowledge we may well have been given these orders after the Nips broke into the Alexandra Hospital and murdered a number of patients in cold blood. At the time we did not know this, but we did know that the Nips were not far away as all their mortar fire was going over us; it was however a beautiful sunny Singapore morning and in our little 'vacuum' it seemed incredibly peaceful. Our job of destroying the stocks of liquor (all very high class stuff) was indeed one of the 'horrors of war' and the fumes given off were so overpowering that we had to take it in turns to come out of the store and get some fresh air through our lungs. [*On the afternoon of 14 February Japanese soldiers broke into the Alexandra Hospital and, ignoring the Red Cross flags and insignia, proceeded to shoot and bayonet about fifty staff and patients. They also took away another 200 who were massacred the following morning; only around six survived. In view of the timings, I suspect that the order to destroy the alcohol stocks may not have been in response to the attack on the hospital.*]

In the early afternoon of Sunday 15 February, Dobbie (my CO) and I were summoned to fortress HQ at Fort Canning to receive Confidential Orders. While we were waiting for these orders we could see that the HQ staff were busy making bonfires of official papers and we felt sure that the worst was about to happen, ie that Singapore was about to surrender. And, sure enough, those were our Orders; 'Ceasefire' to take effect, if I remember rightly, at 8.00 pm that evening. We drove back to BSD both feeling that the bottom had fallen out of our world; we had thought that once the Causeway was blown there would be a real 'last ditch' battle for the Island and we had braced ourselves accordingly. Wavell's Special Order of the Day had reinforced this feeling, yet here we were giving in when large numbers of troops (a fair number, admittedly, second line) had never been engaged against the Japanese. However, one heartening sight as we drove back along Connaught Drive was, as it seemed, all the 25 pounder guns on the Island lined up wheel to wheel along the Padang, all blazing away for all they were worth, obviously determined that if they must surrender (and 'spike' their guns) they would not do so until they had fired off every last round of ammunition.

We drove back to our unit and passed on our orders for implementing the surrender, which was due to take effect that evening. After dark we searched the Harbour Board waterfront for a craft in which to try to escape to Sumatra, but all we could find was a steel ship's lifeboat on a partially submerged tug alongside the harbour wall. By the time we managed to man-handle her into the harbour, find sails and oars and provision her dawn was breaking and the tide had turned against us (which would have swept us straight back towards the Japanese lines). All of this made us feel that our venture had become unacceptably hazardous; by that evening the Nips had occupied our part of the SHB, which put paid to any hopes we had of getting away under cover of darkness that night. With the benefit of hindsight, there was an outside chance of getting to Sumatra (across which an escape route to the west coast [*at Padang*] had been set up) if we had been able to get a tow from a launch, several of which had got away from Singapore around that time. On balance however the odds were very much against us, even allowing for the fact that for 24 hours after the actual surrender there was very little activity by the Nips. This was probably a natural reaction, one now realises, after they had achieved a major victory in capturing Singapore with, as we now know, a relatively limited force.

Before I go on to describe the next three and a half years that I spent as a guest of His Imperial Japanese Majesty in Changi and on the Burma-Siam Railway, it is appropriate here to give an outline of Bobbie's experiences after we said goodbye to each other on Collyer Quay on 30 January, as hers is quite a story in itself.

[I will now let Bobbie tell this part of the story herself, in the form of a letter that she wrote in Melbourne in June 1943, shortly after she heard for the first time that Richard (Dickie, as she called him) was a prisoner of war (although she of course had no idea whether or not he was still alive). The letter describes, in some detail, what happened after she said goodbye to Richard in Singapore on 30 January 1942 until she managed to get to Australia in March 1942. The letter was never posted; the only letters that could be sent to PoWs were 25-word Red Cross letters. Over the course of the war she sent twenty-seven of these letters to Richard (all of which he received), but she never received any communication from him; she did not know he was still alive until after the Japanese surrender in September 1945. She eventually handed her 'Melbourne letters' to Richard when they finally met up in Colombo in October 1945.]

[*Letter from Bobbie to Richard*]

Melbourne
6 June 1943

Darling,

These will be letters I cannot post to you. When we are together again there will be so much to tell each other it will be difficult to know where to begin.

I was so sure I would see you again before I left on the Sunday I felt quite cheerful. If only I had known I would have made you stay with me a little longer! I never thought Singapore would not hold and was sure I was going to Java for a few months and would return – silly of me I suppose and I have wondered since if you had some inkling of what was to come as you kept telling me not to stay in Java but to carry on to Australia. I insisted I would stay in Java near you and I was only there two weeks. Dearest, I hope you have not been worried thinking perhaps I was caught in the 'bag' there.

The night before we left one of the other girls from the office and I decided to sleep on camp beds in the office in case we were unable to get a conveyance early the following morning. We made ourselves pretty comfortable, but had not been in bed long before the old siren went and then the whistles in the building joined in the symphony. Mavis and I stayed put for a while then snooped out on the balcony to see what we could see. We were facing the aerodrome and of course there was a fire there; they were dive bombing. It was quite a short raid and off the monkeys went. You may not remember it, but the night of 31 was about a full moon. Mavis and I stood on the balcony gazing at Singapore spread out below so sharply and clearly, and in the distance the sea shimmered like a piece of silver cloth; we both felt sad at the thought of leaving the next day – it all seemed (alas it was only a mirage) so peaceful. Back to bed and a surprisingly quiet night.

Some lads in a flat above, who were also going to Java, invited us up for breakfast. In the midst of which (8.30) we got a message from the Police to get down to the wharf at once as the ship was going to sail earlier than anticipated. We hurled ourselves in the waiting cars and tore down to the jetty, only to find a submarine parked where our ship should have been! No sign of any vessel. The wharf was strewn with drums, containing petrol I believe! We hadn't been there long when 'Moaning Minnie' started to sing [*the Air Raid siren*]. Everyone rushed round in circles; there was practically nothing in the way of shelters and I remember having a brief argument with one of the girls as to whether a small railway track, about a foot below ground level, was a good shelter or not. In the midst of it a man called out to us that there was a shelter further on. Off we ran; the shelter was made of mud and coal dust and was packed, so we sat on the steps. Eventually the 'All Clear' went; nothing had come anywhere near us. Still no ship to be seen so the 'Blokes in Authority' decided that an exposed wharf was not the best place for thousands of females and children and we were ordered to proceed to the Station 'just a few yards down the road'. This proved to be at least a mile off, and we were told that we would be warned in good time to come back. At the Station the lads in our party (we were 10 – 5 of each) managed to obtain some more than welcome coffee and biscuits. We were feeling somewhat hot and tired by now. There was a raid while we were at the Station; I don't think it was very near but we were all lying about on the floor trying to get under benches! The man next to me took off his tin hat and insisted on my wearing it; I refused and we had a bit of an argument – finally he banged it on my head. (Secretly I was rather thrilled to be wearing a tin hat! Do you remember how badly I wanted one?) At mid-day we were told to go back to the wharf as the ship was sailing soon; arrived – no ship. At 4.15 the ship came alongside and we heaved our luggage on board (I was able to take everything with me), and lined up to have accommodation allotted. Being 'Government' we girls got cabins (third class) so we gave our blankets and pillows to the lads (who had not brought any of their own). They slept on the hatch near our baggage. At about 6.30 we sailed. (A rather trying day.) I was properly equipped for such a day having furnished myself with a navy blue siren suit for just such an occasion. [*This was a Dutch ship, with a Dutch captain who, Bobbie later recalled, did not particularly relish his involvement with the British in their war against the Japanese.*]

If I go on telling you about everything in such detail I shall never reach the end of the story, but that day is rather vivid in my memory. We were very lucky and had no trouble at all sailing to Palembang. A ship had been sunk that morning in the mouth of the river and the Captain said that had we sailed at the right time from Singapore, we would have shared the same fate. We eventually got to Batavia on 6th Feb, and I immediately sent you a cable and an airmail letter. Did you ever get them? We arrived in Batavia on Friday night in time for dinner, and reported for work the next morning at 9.00. It was a bit shattering but there was a lot to be done.

7 June 1943

The office in Batavia consisted of one tiny room and we all crowded into it somehow; fortunately we were never all there at one time as there were not sufficient chairs to go round. The place was air-conditioned and absolutely freezing; outside was boiling hot and the result was that I got one of the worst colds I've had. We stayed at the 'Des Indes' Hotel, a wonderful place. It was packed to overflowing. We had a large double room with two single beds and five camp beds. To share a bathroom (a most gorgeous tiled affair) with only six others after sharing with literally hundreds on the ship was the acme of luxury. After a few days the Office decided to take a house for us girls and let us run a Mess. All very nice in theory, but in practice we nearly went nuts. It took us 15 minutes by taxi to get to the office, and our servants could neither speak nor understand any language we could. We didn't know where any shops were and Batavia is very spread out. We got little Malay/Javanese/English books and I used to make out lists of menus for the Boy; the result was frightful and the meals uneatable! After that we used simply to hand over some money to the Boy and indicate how many would be in. This scheme worked extremely well, although we were hardly ever in for dinner. I met an awfully nice young lad who was kindness itself to me. He took me out to dinner almost every night and in the end it was he who took me down to the ship out of Batavia and got all my luggage on board. [*This was Brian Ogley of BOAC (British Overseas Airways Corporation) who had been in Singapore as BOAC's representative, and who Richard had known through various business dealings in 1939/40.*]

After the fall of Singapore the Office had asked me what I wanted to do; they were getting everyone away they could and only keeping a skeleton staff in Java. The Boss said if I wanted to go it would be no bad reflection on me, and said that the man I worked under in Singapore had told him that I had behaved very well there! I said I would like to go to India if I could have a job there, but he told me that there was nothing available. I thought and thought, and finally decided I had better push off while I could still take my goods and chattels with me. I had no objections to staying if we really were going to be able to stay in Java, but just to hang on for a couple of weeks and then to get out with the proverbial toothbrush seemed rather silly. I said that I would like to go to

Australia and was told that my passage would be arranged. It was difficult getting a passage to Australia as everything seemed to be making for India. However a berth was obtained on a dreadful little ship (I later discovered it was an old China River Boat – horrors). But Brian, who had been trying to persuade me to get out of Java, rang up one morning and said he knew of a good ship going to Australia and had booked a passage for me on her, so that was alright [*this was the* Marella]. I was told to keep in touch with the shipping office as they could not state a sailing time. Brian suddenly appeared at the house after dinner one night (all the other girls living at the Mess had gone, the last one having left that day). He said that the ship was leaving early next morning, and he himself was leaving for Tjilatjap [*on the south coast of Java*] at six o'clock next morning; he insisted on seeing me actually on board the ship as he was convinced I would miss it otherwise. He said that he had arranged for a car to be at 'Des Indes' where he was staying at 3 o'clock, so I decided the best thing was for me to spend the night there too. I got to bed at midnight, and up again at 2.45. We piled all my stuff into the taxi and drove off to the docks, where we had a terrible job to find the ship. We had no permits or passes and wandered all over the place. At one time I thought we were going to be arrested, and when I think back on it, it surprises me that some zealous Dutch sentry didn't take a pot shot at us. Eventually we located the ship after I had nearly given up all hope; Brian had to go straight back. I sat on a deserted promenade deck and watched the sunrise feeling very miserable and forlorn; somehow I felt as if I was leaving everything I really cared for behind me. The rest of the passengers came on later. Some members of the native crew refused to sail and they were pushed on board by soldiers – poor devils. Actually we didn't sail until six o'clock that evening, 20th February. We were convoyed, and all felt nervous about the Sunda Strait [*between Sumatra and Java*] as the Japanese fleet was at Palembang. There was a thunderstorm that night which woke me up – thought we were being bombed. We got through the Strait alright and then left the convoy and proceeded on our own. [*Their convoy escort was the cruiser HMS* Exeter. *A week later, on 27 February,* Exeter *was badly damaged during the Battle of the Java Sea, and two days later on 1 March was sunk while attempting to escape through the Sunda Strait. Of the 652 members of her ship's company who survived the sinking, 152 were to die in Japanese PoW camps.*] I slept practically all the time for four days. Although I didn't feel tired when I first got on board, I must have been pretty worn out. Luckily I had a single cabin to myself on the Promenade Deck, about ten yards from my Boat Station. Never have I felt less interest in my fellow passengers than I did on that voyage with the exception of an extremely nice lady from Malaya who sat at the Captain's table with me.

After leaving Fremantle crossing the Australian Bight we had it dreadfully rough; I thought the ship was going to sink. Everything seemed to be loose, furniture was running around, the trunks in my cabin just rolled from one end of the room to the other and crockery was smashed to bits. The heavy weather started in the middle of the night and it was so black it seemed to press against you. In due course we got to Melbourne, all in one piece.

[*Bobbie subsequently went on to Sydney by train, where she stayed with her mother's sister. Ten days after arriving in Sydney she received a telegram from MEW offering her a job in Melbourne, which she accepted. So began an arduous but interesting three and a half years with the SOE, known in Australia as the Services Reconnaissance Department (SRD) and in India and Ceylon as Force 136. Her SOE Service Number was A/K100; she served as secretary to Lieutenant Colonel Egerton Mott, the head of the SRD mission in Melbourne from March 1942 to July 1945, and as secretary to the head of the Malayan Country Section of Force 136 in Colombo from August to December 1945. Quite a 'war record'.*]

Chapter Three

Prisoner of War – Changi
February 1942 to April 1943

I started my time as a POW in style by driving a 3 ton 4-wheel drive Marmon-Harrington truck out from SHB to Changi, loaded down with all the rations we could cram onto it; this was in accordance with Nip orders allowing certain limited rations to be taken out to Changi in trucks to be driven only by officers. Otherwise a depressing journey; long columns of our troops trailing out to Changi (some 12 to 15 miles away) with the local inhabitants watching, glum and wooden-faced, their world having been shattered as much, or even more than ours by the surrender of the 'impregnable fortress'. That night we bivouacked where we could in the Changi Barracks area. I well remember bumping into Ralph Prince of 'The Loyals' [*The Loyal Regiment (North Lancashire)*] on Castle Hill. Ralph, in addition to the prevailing gloom, was pretty well exhausted physically, having marched the whole way out to Changi from The Loyals' battle position in the Alexandra area. In those first few days in Changi water was extremely short, particularly on that first night, but fortunately I had a full water-bottle, generously laced with whisky – a compensation for the sad duty of having to break up the stocks of liquor in the Medical Comforts Store at Alexandra some two or three days before. Ralph and I shared this 'Medical Comfort' and both felt a lot better for it. I was particularly glad to be of service to Ralph in this way as he and his wife Leila (also a Shanghai girl) had very generously put Bobbie up when she was in Singapore in June 1940 for Sherwood Connor and Betty Gordon's wedding (the wedding at which we had met).

In the early days at Changi we all got a number of 'shocks to the system'; perhaps the most severe shock was the firm order from the Nips that in future we must live on the same diet as the Asiatics, that is basically rice, but in our case with very little of the meat and vegetables which can do so much to make a rice diet palatable (to western tastes). This sudden change of diet caused various digestive troubles, starting with severe constipation for two or three weeks which then went to the other extreme of diarrhoea. The next problem was lack of water as many of the water mains had been damaged or sabotaged in the course of the fighting; fortunately the Nips had allowed some Public Works Department personnel to remain at liberty and, thanks to their efforts, water supplies were restored to a reasonable level relatively quickly. In addition all surplus rainwater from the tropical storms which occurred from time to time was carefully husbanded. The luxury of bathing only occurred when there was a particularly heavy rain-storm and one could have a real wash under an over-flowing gutter. The other thing one missed so badly was the lack of news from the outside world; in those days I was considered a dangerous pessimist for expressing the view that it would be at least six months before we were free (in the event what an blooming optimist I was!). It was only after about a month when odd working parties went into Singapore and were able to establish contacts with the Chinese that we got to know the full extent of Japanese conquests in the Far East. When I heard that the Dutch East Indies had gone, I was glad that when we said 'goodbye' I had urged Bobbie to keep on going down to Australia which, with one or two pauses on the way, she did indeed do. My urgings could not greatly influence events as it turned out, but for some reason I never had any doubt that she would get through. When I got her first Red Cross letter from Australia a year or more later I was not surprised (such was my strange faith in her lucky star), but I was indeed surprised and delighted that she had taken the trouble to write to me.

Prisoner of War – Changi February 1942 to April 1943 71

For the first fortnight or so I was with a whole gaggle of officers in a delightfully situated Senior Officer's Quarter at Fairy Point immediately overlooking the entrance to the Straits of Johore and the Singapore Naval Base. I have three recollections of this period. Firstly, one of our batmen cleaning out our dormitory knocked over a bottle of 'Black and White' whisky which Dobbie and I had taken in with us; this shattered on the tile floor and provided a striking demonstration of what a lot of liquid there is in a bottle of whisky when spread out on a highly polished floor, not to mention the overpowering aroma. Secondly, the Japanese Battle Fleet (less aircraft carriers) steaming up the Straits of Johore to the Naval Base; beautiful looking ships and very business-like. They sailed shortly afterwards and took part in support of the carrier-borne attack on Trincomalee and Colombo. The main British naval forces had withdrawn westwards and the only sizeable naval units to be caught were, sadly, the old carrier HMS *HERMES* and the two cruisers HMS *CORNWALL* and HMS *DEVONSHIRE*. The third recollection is of eye-witness reports from some of our people who were nearby of lorry-loads of Chinese being made to march into the sea at Changi point where the Nips mowed them down with machine guns. After the Nips had departed, some of the bodies were recovered from the sea and one man was found to be still alive. He was taken into our hospital in Roberts Barracks (Changi) where he made a good recovery, and was taken onto the strength as a Eurasian member of the Straits Settlement Volunteer Force. Great care was however taken that he remained in the Camp (no outside working parties) and that as far as possible he had no contact with the Nips. The Chinese executed at Changi Point were alleged Communists; some of them probably were, but in the drag-net operations conducted by the Nips at this time a lot of innocent people were probably caught up.

After a month or so we all shook down in the Changi area which was quite extensive with, by POW standards, reasonable accommodation; very crowded at first, but easier after various working parties were despatched into Singapore to assist in the clearing up of bomb damage etc. The unit organisations and command structure were retained as far as possible and so 'Base Supply Depot' carried on with Dobbie as CO and myself as Adjutant, which gave us a nominal something to do although we did not have much in the way of supplies to distribute.

BSD was housed in the former MT Workshop (a fairly high-roofed single storey building) and a low single storey building which had formerly been the Workshop Offices. The Workshop itself was used as accommodation for the Other Ranks and for the storage of such supplies as were available, while the offices were Officers' accommodation. From time to time one of the BSD officers (T.B. Rogers), who from civilian life in the Import/Export business had a fluent command of Bazaar Malay, was allowed to go into Singapore with the Nips on local purchase expeditions and was able to come back with various 'goodies' which he obtained from pre-war Chinese business connections. At this time the Nips were 'on the crest of the wave' and fairly easy going. For a time these expeditions were our main source of news of the outside world, and not very encouraging news at that!

The purchase of these 'goodies' had been financed out of the Officers' own pockets and went to be cooked in the cookhouse which was common to Officers and ORs; the cooks no doubt got their cut but the main bulk of the ORs did not. I felt very strongly that it was all wrong for Officers to be guzzling good food in close proximity to a lot of very hungry ORs and I refused to have any part in the feasts in the Officers' Quarters. My only concession to this racket was one bottle of Carlsberg beer on a Sunday morning; a treat which was only available for 5 or 6 weeks.

It was at about this time that Guy le Mesurier, an elderly (probably 55 to 60) Emergency Commissioned RASC officer of considerable charm, started up a still on Temple Hill where he lived in a tent in glorious isolation. He had, I believe, worked as a prospector or

Prisoner of War – Changi February 1942 to April 1943   73

surveyor in isolated areas in many parts of the world and claimed that wherever he may have been he had always been self-sufficient for liquor. Changi POW Camp was no exception; any vegetable refuse from the kitchens around the place went into the pot, and he produced a clear 'gin' which, when mixed with fresh lime juice (when available) made a very acceptable 'Gimlet'. The money he obtained from selling his gin enabled him to treat himself to various small luxuries, but he did eventually die of cirrhosis of the liver, having in the meantime been a great benefactor to the community. I think he knew where he was heading and had no great desire to see the post-war world. Incidentally, the actor John le Mesurier, very similar in looks to Guy, took the part of the Sergeant in the 'Dad's Army' TV series and I always feel that he must have been a relative of Guy's. [*Basil Guy le Mesurier was a member of a very extensive Guernsey family, and it is unlikely that he was directly related to John le Mesurier. Guy was born in Exeter in 1889, and became a gas and chemical engineer (useful in the distilling business!). He died in captivity on 1 July 1945.*] Guy's gin was still available when we got back from 'F' Force [*see Chapter 4*] at the end of 1943 and we really felt that we had got back to civilisation when we found that we could still get our Sunday morning 'Gimlet'. It must have been shortly after this that Guy died; sadly that was the end of POW Sunday morning 'Gimlets'!

In the early days in Changi various humorous stories, probably suitably embroidered, were going the rounds which, at a time when news was patchy and unreliable, helped to sustain morale. Some examples:

1. In the last hours before Singapore fell the Banks were ordered to destroy all Straits Settlements currency notes; an AIF [*Australian Imperial Force*] party was detailed to go to one of the Dutch banks to assist in this work. On enquiring from the Dutch bank officials whether these notes were of any value they were told 'No', and that they were welcome to keep a few as 'souvenirs'. On arrival

back at Changi these 'souvenirs' (in denominations of anything up to $100) were used as counters in the many poker schools which had started up, and quite considerable sums of 'money' changed hands. Great was the heart-burning and furious disputes when the first working parties returned from Singapore city with the news that the Straits Settlements currency was still very much legal tender. Not only that, it was in fact very much preferred by the Chinese to the Japanese 'Banana Money', a situation which prevailed right up to the end of the war – a striking illustration of the faith of the local population in eventual Allied victory.
2. When units first moved into Changi they all took with them as many British tinned rations as they could carry, with orders that on arrival in Changi they should be handed in to a central Supply organisation for the benefits of the whole camp. These orders were, naturally, somewhat reluctantly obeyed and at least one unit was known to have considerable stocks of rations which had not been handed in. Searches for these rations failed to reveal them until a Supply Officer made a final call on the CO of the unit concerned. As on previous occasions the Supply Officer was courteously received by the CO and his Adjutant sitting at improvised tables in the Orderly Room. It was only on this last visit that the Supply Officer realised that the Orderly Room 'tables' were in fact old doors or table-tops supported at either end on packing cases of tinned rations.
3. A lot of thieving of Japanese stores had been taking place at one of the work camps on Singapore Island, so the whole camp was paraded for a lecture by a Senior Japanese Officer on the iniquities of stealing from His Imperial Japanese Majesty. For this purpose the Senior Japanese Officer drove onto the parade ground in a lorry and stood on the back to deliver his harangue. When the time came to drive away, the lorry refused to start since while he was speaking all the petrol had been syphoned out of the tank.

The usual round of camp activities (gardening, reading and courses at the Changi 'University' – for which there were some highly qualified teachers) was interrupted in September 1942 by a demand from the Nips that we should all sign a 'no escape' undertaking. Refusal to do this resulted in orders from the Nips that we should

The Laird Brothers, Brooklands, 1934. Richard, left, and Henry, right.

Their sister, Maudie Gatey (née Laird) in 1930.

Bobbie Couper Patrick, Shanghai 1935.

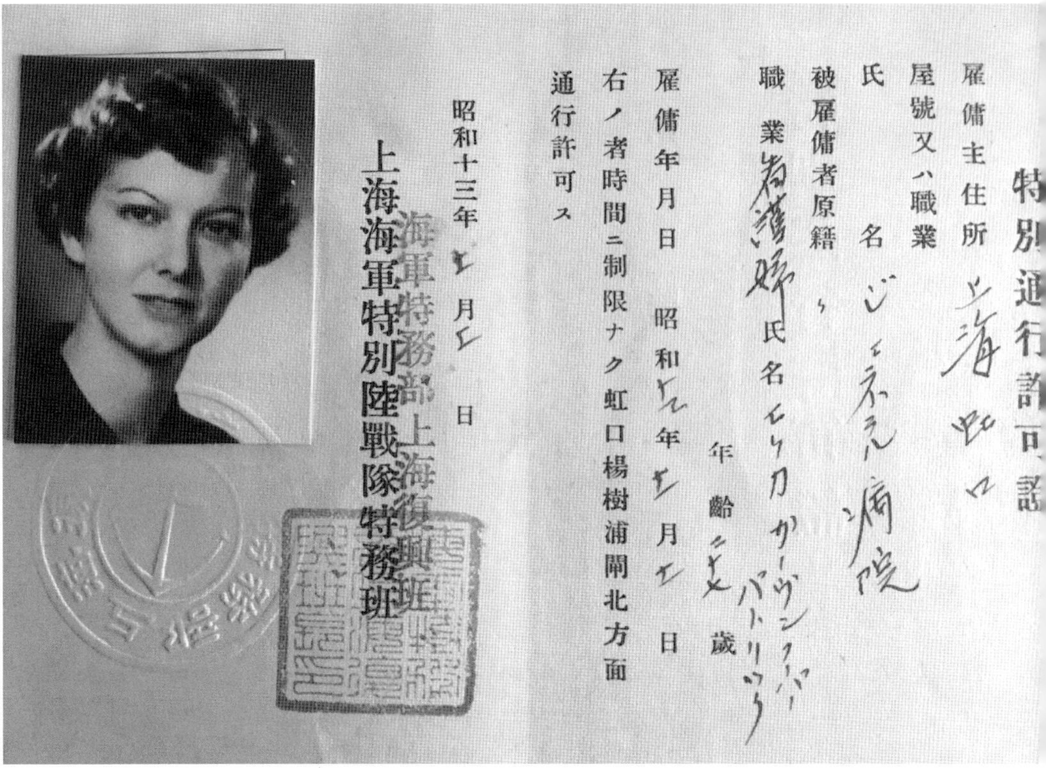

(*Above*) Japanese Pass issued to Bobbie Couper Patrick 1937, to permit travel to the Japanese section of the International Settlement (where her parents lived).

(*Below*) China United Apartments, Bubbling Well Road, Shanghai 1937.

(*Above*) Former China United Apartments, now the Pacific Hotel, 2011.

(*Below*) Shanghai, The Bund, in 1937.

Japanese Cruiser HIJNS *Idzumo* at her berth near the Japanese Consulate.

Sentry Post on Elgin Road, Shanghai, close to 'Windy Corner'.

Part of No.3 Section, Shanghai Scottish, at 'Windy Corner' August 1937 (Richard Laird is second from the left).

Shanghai Scottish returning to billets from the line at 'Windy Corner'.

Shell damage outside Shanghai Scottish billets on Elgin Road, Shanghai.

The Racecourse from China United Apartments. Shanghai Municipal Buses are parked on the Racecourse for safety.

(*Above*) HMS *Suffolk* approaching the British Naval Buoys in the Whampoa River. (Photograph taken from the Sun Insurance office at No.1 The Bund)

(*Below*) Chapei set on fire by the retreating Chinese. The godown in the centre of the picture is where a Chinese battalion made their final stand. (Photograph taken from the China United Apartments)

North Station, Shanghai, after the Chinese withdrawal. The iron fence in the foreground is the boundary of the International Settlement.

Zig-zag on the Uchikongo Electric Railway, showing one of the sidings used to reverse the direction of travel as the train ascended or descended the mountain.

Mai-mai Ross and Richard Laird at Umi Kongo.

The Diamond Mountains.

Group at the Kume Mountain Hut. Ian Aucott, left; Count Stefano Macchi di Cellere, centre; Richard Laird, right.

Bobbie Couper Patrick and Richard Laird, Bridesmaid and Best Man, at the wedding of Sherwood Connor and Betty Gordon, Singapore, 20 June 1940.

(*Above*) Sherwood Connor, Betty Gordon, 'Sandy' Gordon (Betty's father) and Douglas Johnston (Betty's cousin), Singapore, 19 June 1940.

(*Below left*) Bobbie in Melbourne 1942. This was the photograph Richard received just before he left for the Burma Railway in April 1943.

(*Below right*) Reverse of this photograph.

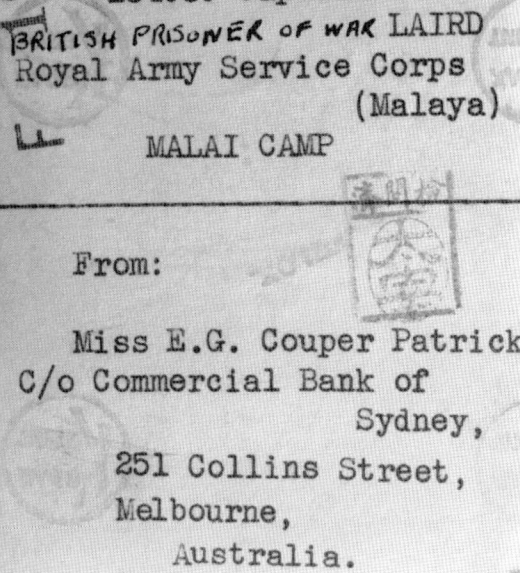

(*Above*) Selarang Barracks, Changi, during the 'Selarang Incident' in September 1942. This photograph is one of a number taken by an Australian, Private George Aspinall, with the folding Six-20 Kodak Brownie camera that he smuggled into captivity. He eventually had to destroy the camera when Japanese searches became increasingly thorough, but he hid the processed negatives in a toilet borehole at Changi Jail; they were returned to him after the war. (Australian War Memorial)

(*Below*) Officer prisoners of war in Changi, 1944. Photograph taken by Major Kennedy Burnside, AAMC. (Australian War Memorial)

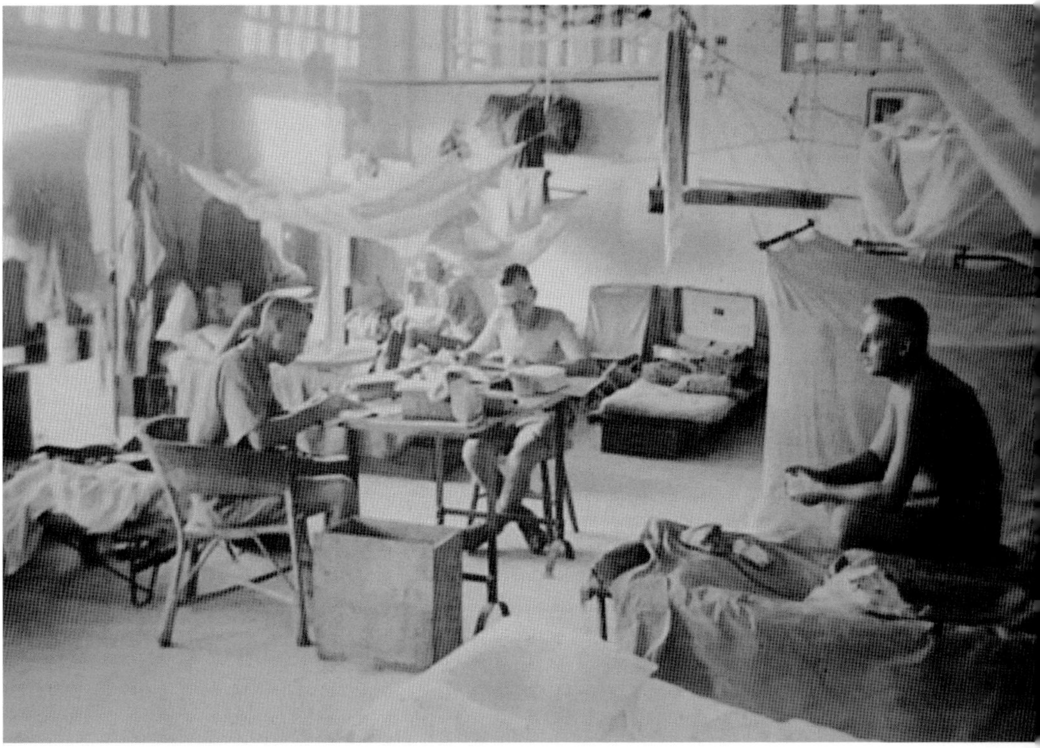

(*Above*) A well-constructed prisoner of war bamboo and attap hut at Kanchanaburi, 1944. Huts in the Railway work camps were similar, but much less 'luxurious'. On arrival at Songkurai, the prisoners found the huts roofless, and the floors a sea of mud. (Australian War Memorial)

(*Below*) Prisoners of war at work on one of the bridges on the Burma Railway, 1943/44. (Australian War Memorial)

(*Above*) Cholera hospital at Songkurai No.1 Camp (five kilometres south of Richard's camp, Songkurai No.2). To the right of the tents is a makeshift operating table. The tent behind is the morgue. This is another George Aspinall photograph. (Australian War Memorial)

(*Below*) Three Australian prisoners of war at Songkurai No.1 Camp classed as 'Fit for Work'. The distended stomach of the man on the right is due to the fact he is suffering from beri-beri. The image, with the tops of the mens' heads chopped off, is exactly as it was taken (clandestinely) by George Aspinall. It is included as it is one of the very few photographs in existence that show the reality of the physical condition of the prisoners in the upper work camps on the Burma Railway. (Australian War Memorial)

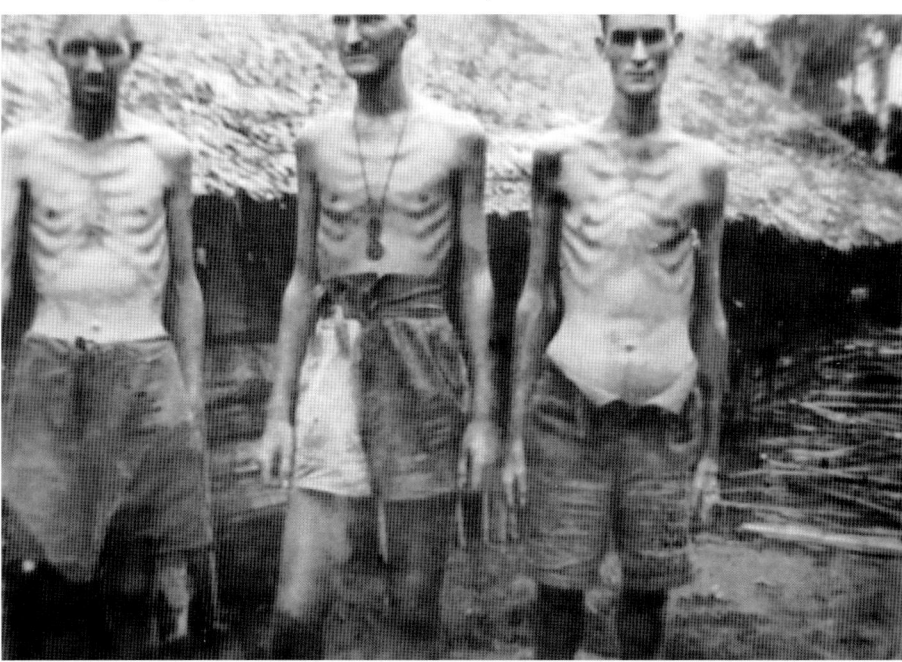

(*Above*) Prisoners of war on a washing platform in a stream at Songkurai No.3 Camp. The last of the George Aspinall photographs in this section. (Australian War Memorial)

(*Below*) Commonwealth War Graves personnel at the Three Pagodas Pass, October 1945. (Australian War Memorial)

(*Above left*) Major Bruce Hunt, Australian Army Medical Corps, Medical Officer I/C Tanbaya Hospital Camp, 1943.

(*Above right*) Lieutenant Colonel Cyril Wild, Ox and Bucks Light Infantry. 'F' Force Japanese Interpreter. 'The Tall Man Who Never Slept'.

(*Left*) Richard Laird (and a nurse) at 107 British General Hospital, Bangalore, October 1945, six weeks after release from Changi.

(*Above left*) Richard's Discharge Certificate from the Army.

(*Above right*) War Office letter granting Richard the honorary rank of captain.

(*Below left and right*) Richard and Bobbie, Return to Singapore in happier times, 1946.

(*Above*) Forty Years On – Singapore Royal Artillery (Volunteers) Reunion, 3 May 1985. Standing, L to R: Cecil Colchester, Eric Henton, George Keyzar, Tommy Thompson, Lincoln Page, John Hosgood, Joe Potter, Frank Lane, Richard Laird, Charles Butterfield, Bill Dobbs, James Barton, Arnold Thorne, Ted Chaplin. Seated, L to R: Pat Sladden, John Richardson, Johnny Johnson, Tiger Coltart, Pat Shaw.

(*Left*) A page from Richard Laird's original hand-written memoir.

all be concentrated in the Selarang Barracks area with only such rations as we could carry with us, and that we should there reflect on our ways and our ingratitude to His Imperial Japanese Majesty. Selarang Barracks had in peacetime housed one British battalion, and now some 16,000 of us were concentrated in this area. I worked out at the time that the area available per man for all purposes (sleeping, eating, cooking, sanitary, hygiene and medical) was 1.5 square yards; this included the barrack square and all floors of the barrack blocks, including the roofs and staircases.

This affair became known later as the 'Selarang Incident' and lasted, as I recall, some 3 or 4 days. After two days during which we maintained our refusal to sign, the Nips, in order to show that they meant business, mounted machine guns on a building commanding the barrack square and took the COs of the British and Australian contingents down to the beach at Changi to witness the execution of four escapees (two British and two Australian) whom they had picked up. The executions were carried out by Indian National Army (INA) personnel who were far from efficient at their job. The use of INA personnel for these executions was, of course, a calculated act on the part of the Nips to humiliate us – not very successful. I heard reliably that the bearing of the four men executed was exemplary, which made the whole botched affair even more sickening for our COs who were forced to witness it. It was after this, and on the advice of our MOs about the rapidly deteriorating health situation in the desperately overcrowded conditions at Selarang, that the COs authorised us to sign the 'paroles' 'under duress'. That done we returned to our quarters after 3 or 4 days to find that the two or three individuals who had volunteered to sign early on, and who had been allowed by the Nips to return to their own quarters, had spent the time ransacking the possessions left behind by those who had gone to Selarang. It did not take long to identify the culprits who were suitably dealt with by our own people.

From the Nip point of view the object of the exercise was that if they did subsequently catch any escapees they could make it much worse for them for having broken a 'solemn oath'. They also demanded similar 'no escape' undertakings from POWs up-country, and in Borneo and the Dutch East Indies. They all, without so far as one knows any contact with Changi, took the same line and only signed 'under duress'.

In, I think, August 1942 (shortly before the 'Selarang Incident') the *ASAMA MARU* (a Nippon Yusen Kaisha liner of some 17,000 tons) called at Singapore on her way back from repatriating Diplomatic personnel to South Africa. She brought with her some 1,800 tons of Red Cross supplies which were offloaded at Singapore. Another officer (Desmond Shean), myself and two ORs were detailed to go into Singapore (where we were billeted in River Valley Road Camp) to supervise the offloading of the Red Cross stores. We checked them into the SHB godowns and found that the shortages from pilfering etc were negligible. These were the last Red Cross stores that we saw until very near the end (ie a full three years) when the Nips, having evidently 'seen the writing on the wall', starting releasing Red Cross foodstuffs which they had evidently been sitting on for some time, some of them, as I knew from the evidence of my own eyes, having been offloaded from the *ASAMA MARU*.

The stay in River Valley Road Camp, although not as comfortable as Changi, made a welcome break from the Changi routine; it was here that a friend (Sheldrake) from 18th Division RASC, introduced me to his 'canary' – a radio concealed in an old ration box with the aerial skilfully concealed in the attap roof of the ration store. Two or more years later (long after the original occupants had left River Valley Road) the Nips discovered the wiring in the roof of the ration store and Sheldrake was sent for and all of us who were in the know feared the worst. However he came back after a few days, very subdued, but none the worse physically; he never did say how he managed to wriggle out of that one.

Also in the River Valley Road camp was Bill Goode, of the Malayan Civil Service, who was later to become Sir William Goode, the last Colonial Governor of Singapore before Independence. In River Valley Road days he was an OR in the Singapore Straits Volunteer Force and I remember very clearly an outstanding lecture which he gave about the Malaya he had known in pre-war days. In that lecture he brought out features which make Malaya such a delightful country; features which I had been subconsciously aware of, but never, until then, fully appreciated. I never subsequently met Bill until the 1960s when he retired and came to live in Streatley-on-Thames [*where Richard and Bobbie also lived*]; sadly he is no longer with us, having died since I started writing these memoirs.

After the 'Selarang Incident' life at Changi was fairly routine except that parties were constantly moving out of Changi to destinations at that time unknown; as we later discovered, they went to Thailand, Sumatra, Borneo and islands in the Dutch East Indies. All of them were more or less bad, but the smaller and more isolated camps were the worst because the Nips were, for practical reasons, unsupervised by their own POW Administration which, at best, was a poor relation in the Japanese military hierarchy. In Changi we even played a St Andrew's Day rugger match on 30th November 1942 in which I (ex-Shanghai Scottish!) represented Scotland; sadly we were narrowly beaten by the 'auld enemy'. We also had a Unit Soccer League, in which I played for the BSD. By the end of the year we had moved over to a block of Married Quarters (where I had been quartered during my 'Embodiment' with the Singapore Royal Artillery (Volunteer) in July 1940). This was near the Royal Artillery barrack block, and it was here that we fairly regularly saw copies (from earlier in the year) of the *Syonan Shimbum*, a Japanese sponsored English-language newspaper printed by the former Singapore Free Press and presented in the same format. These papers described in some detail the bitter naval actions in the Solomon Islands in 'The Slot' (the stretch of water between two parallel strings of islands which make up the Solomon Islands), which became known as 'Iron Bottom Sound' because so many ships were sunk there. At that time we had our own regular 'News service' and frankly refused to believe the Japanese claims in the *Syonan Shimbum* of the number of American ships sunk. In fact history has shown that the Japanese claims of American losses were not far wrong, however they minimised their own losses and never admitted to their own people the infinitely greater capacity of the Americans to make good the losses which they had sustained. This applied equally to aircraft, and particularly to pilots, as well as to ships. I often wished that I had kept the odd copy of *Syonan Shimbum*, although I fear it would not have survived 'F' Force which is the next chapter in this story.

[In about June 1942 Bobbie, by then working for the Services Reconnaissance Department (the Australian arm of SOE) in Melbourne, started writing 25-word Red Cross letters to Richard (Dickie) although she did not at that time know if he was a prisoner of war, or indeed if he was still alive. Dickie received these letters, and the photographs she sent of herself (normally about 9 to 12 months after she had sent them). She eventually discovered that he was a POW a year later in June 1943. Extracts from letters she wrote in June 1943 describe how this happened, and give an insight into the stress of not having any reliable news as to the fate of friends and loved ones.]

[*Extract of a letter from Bobbie to Richard (Dickie)*]

Melbourne
6 June 1943

Darling,

Two or three days ago I got news that you are a prisoner! Dickie, that was the first bit of news I had had about you of any description since we said 'Au Revoir' on Collyers Quay on 30th January 1942 – such a very long time to wait. At times I used to feel quite desperate wondering if I would ever get news of you. The moment I got to Sydney I went to the Red Cross about you, but came up against a brick wall as I was no relation of yours. However a cousin of mine knew someone and he promised to try and find out for me, but without success. I asked all sorts of men whom I knew had got out at the very end, but no luck. Last October I sent an Air Mail letter (ordinary letters to England sometimes take four months) to the man I worked for in Singapore and asked him if he could find out anything for me, but I never heard from him so obviously either my letter or his reply had become a casualty as I know he would have answered my letter. Then Betty [*Betty Connor, at whose marriage Bobbie and Dickie had met in June 1940*] had the bright idea of writing to the 'Sun' [*insurance office*] and asking them for news of you, saying you were a friend of her husband's etc. (As a matter of fact, as a last resort, I was going to write to the 'Sun' myself, as unfortunately I don't know the names or addresses of any of your many sisters.) Betty sent her letter Air Mail and the 'Sun' (nice people) cabled a reply that you were a prisoner, and Betty immediately let me know. Darling, I haven't got words to describe how thrilled and happy I was to hear you were a prisoner; after sixteen months of suspense I at last knew that you were alive. For the last few days I have been wandering around with a silly sort of grin all the time. It's just wonderful, wonderful, wonderful. Ever since we parted you have been so very close to me and I felt you must be alright; how could I have that feeling if you were not in this world too? The night before news of you arrived I dreamt I was in a tram and overheard a conversation between two ladies, one of whom said she had news of you – wasn't that strange?

I have written you regularly once a month for exactly a year now. We are only supposed to write once a month. Some people do it more often, however I have stuck closely to the 'rules' as I do not want to do anything that would react unfavourably on you. The letters seem so wooden but it's hard to know how to make them otherwise in the circumstances, although I have done my best when the news has been very good and I have been tempted to try to tell you so in some camouflaged way, but decided that it was not worth the risk. I wonder how many of my letters you have got?

Hello my Darling, 7 June 1943

Poor Betty has not had any news of Sherwood yet; when she rang me up to tell me about you (as well as sending a telegram) she sounded so tired of waiting to hear about Sherwood. I can understand only too well having gone through the same sense of disappointment at hearing of my friends all getting news and me none. As a matter of fact none of the Volunteer's names, except officers, have come through as yet. [*Betty's husband, Sherwood Connor was a Private in the SSVF (Straits Settlements Volunteer Force, a military reserve force like the Territorial Army) rather than the British Army.*] I wish you were a Colonel! Not for the sake of the rank, but just so that you might perhaps get better treatment; anyway I shall always be thankful that you are an officer. Poor old Sherwood, as a Private it can't be too good. I saw him sometime late in January and I don't think I had seen him so cheery before; I wonder what made him so chirpy? By the way Pop Gordon [*Betty's father*] was interned in Shanghai last November, when the first lot of men were rounded up. Up till January 1943 their camp was quite 'de luxe' (I have not heard of conditions since then) and Pop was very well and cheerful. I told Betty not to worry as he was probably running the place.

8 June 1943

Sweetheart,

Where was I? Oh, I know, Melbourne! I really wanted to see Betty; her cousin, who I managed to contact, told me that she was in hospital, her son George having arrived a week ago. I chartered a taxi and gave him the address – gosh what a long way out it was; I thought that I was being driven half way to Sydney. The taxi driver was a friendly soul and I said that I hoped he was not going to charge me a fortune. He agreed upon 14 shillings to take me there, wait 20 minutes and bring me back, which wasn't too bad for this country. I was scared stiff that they would refuse to let me see Betty; I didn't give my name, and Betty was only told 'a lady to see you'! She gave a loud shriek when she saw me; I was so excited I just talked ten to the dozen. Betty had had a letter from Sherwood early February 1942 in which he told her I had gone to Java. All that happened 15 months ago and Betty is still no wiser now as to Sherwood's fate than she was then.

[*Bobbie was godmother to Betty's son George.*]

Chapter Four

Prisoner of War – 'F' Force and the Burma Railway April to December 1943

*I*n April 1943 the comparatively ordered routine in Changi was abruptly disrupted by Richard's inclusion in a large work party, designated 'F' Force, that was to be dispatched up-country. A number of such parties had already been sent north from Changi, and it was known that they were being employed on the building of a railway in Thailand. This is now commonly known as The Burma Railway. The Japanese built it using prisoners of war and civilian labourers to connect the existing railheads at Ban Pong in Thailand and Thanbyuzayat in Burma, a distance of 415 kilometres, in order to supply their army in Burma. Construction began in June 1942 in Thailand, and shortly afterwards in Burma, and was completed in late October 1943 when the two construction gangs met approximately eighteen kilometres south of the Three Pagodas Pass. It is estimated that its construction cost the lives of over 12,000 Allied prisoners of war and 90,000 civilian labourers.

In April 1943 little was known in Changi about the conditions on The Railway, and the Japanese led the British and Australian military authorities to believe that they would be an improvement on those in Changi. The reality was tragically different, made worse by the fact that 'F' Force was to be deployed to the northernmost section of the railway, over 300 kilometres from the railhead at Ban Pong, where the work camps were primitive in the extreme, and the very wet south west monsoon *was about to break. The Force also included a large number of 'unfit' men.*

The conditions at Songkurai No.2 camp, where Richard was destined to spend his time on The Burma Railway, were described thus by Lionel de Rosario in his book **Nippon Slaves**.

'We stood on the eastern bank and just gazed at a large clearing beyond... . The wet season had begun and it was cold, the rain fell in torrents. To reach the camp we had to cross the fast flowing River Kwai upon a very fragile wooden bridge. The clearing of the camp was covered in a thick carpet of black mud; the attap sided huts had no roofs. This site made us feel utterly dejected... .

The huts were 100 metres long and six metres wide, constructed of bamboo with attap panels in the walls. There was an opening in each wall but no roof, and the floor, as outside, was a mudbath. There was a central aisle with sleeping platforms each side, raised 75cm above the ground and made of bamboo slats... .

The task at Songkurai was to construct a large-span timber bridge, high above and across the River Kwai... . We also had to construct 10 kilometres of track. The task was to be completed within 5 months and the Japanese engineers were determined to achieve their goal.'

One of those engineers, with whom Richard was to cross swords, was Lieutenant Hiroshi Abe. Lieutenant Abe was convicted of war crimes in 1946 and sentenced to death, although this was commuted to fifteen years imprisonment, subsequently reduced to eleven. Unusually, he was one of the few Japanese who, as an older man, faced up to his past. He admitted to having been a war criminal and, having initially denied his responsibility, he eventually, in 1995, called upon his government to apologise fully for the way it treated prisoners. In his statement he added, 'Japan as a nation has not properly considered the issues. Japanese people do not know and do not care what happened. Japan has been preoccupied with economic power.' This was after Abe met one of his former victims, Jim Bradley, whose escape from Songkurai Richard alludes to in his memoir.

James Bradley has described his escape in full in his book **Towards the Setting Sun.** *The escape party, consisting of ten men from a variety of units, including one Indian fisherman, left Songkurai No.2 on 5 July 1943 from the cholera isolation hospital in the camp. The four British survivors were arrested by the Japanese (having been 'sold' by Burmese natives) on 21 August 1943 and taken to Nieke to be executed. There, Major Cyril Wild, the 'F' Force Japanese interpreter, intervened with the local Japanese commander, Lieutenant Colonel Banno, and persuaded him that such an execution would bring everlasting disgrace on the Emperor and the Imperial Japanese Army. They were subsequently tried by Japanese Court Martial in Singapore on trumped up charges and sentenced to eight to nine years imprisonment; they were all brought out of Outram Road jail after two or three months and returned to Changi. Jim Bradley said, 'There can be no doubt that it was Cyril alone who saved our lives.'*

Cyril Wild was one of the outstanding characters of 'F' Force. In pre-war Japan he had learnt not only day-to-day Japanese, but was also fluent in the language of the Imperial Japanese Court. As 'F' Force's interpreter this gave him a unique psychological ascendency over the ordinary Japanese officers, which he used to good effect. After the war Major Cyril Wild, later Lieutenant Colonel, MBE, was appointed as War Crimes Liaison Officer, Malaya and Singapore. In this post he controlled the work of the three War Crimes Investigation Teams operating in that area. He was involved in a number of war crimes trials, and sought out and apprehended over 170 suspected Japanese war criminals. Tragically, he was killed in an air crash on take-off from Kai Tak airport, Hong Kong, on 25 September 1946 aged 38. This was the day before the start of his major war crimes trial, 'F Force, Burma-Siam Railway', in Singapore, the trial that was perhaps *closest to his heart. He knew both the defendants and the witnesses personally, and had lived through the events himself. He was known by the Japanese at Songkurai as 'nemuranu se no takai otoko'* – The Tall Man Who Never Slept. *His narrative report on 'F' Force is reproduced at Appendix I, and his story is told in full by Jim Bradley in his book* Cyril Wild – The Tall Man Who Never Slept.

Because of the very high levels of death and disease in the three Songkurai work camps, a hospital camp was established in August 1943 at Tanbaya, around seventy kilometres further north in Burma, to take men too sick to work out of camps at the northern end of the Railway, because of the difficulty the Japanese had in getting enough food up to those camps. It was eventually evacuated and closed down in January/February 1944. Of the 1,924 sick men sent to Tanbaya during that time, 750 died. Richard was one of those evacuated to Tanbaya in September 1943.

While he was there he came into contact with another of the outstanding characters of 'F' Force. This was Major Bruce Hunt, AAMC (Australian Army Medical Corps) who was born in 1898 and served as a Gunner in the First World War. On returning to Australia he studied medicine in Melbourne before moving to Perth, as a General Physician. On the Railway he was one of the most highly rated medical officers, not just for his medical skills with very limited resources, but of almost greater importance his leadership and willingness and ability to stand up to the Japanese to protect his men from the worst of their excesses. In August 1943 he was sent to Tanbaya as the senior MO. Here, amongst other things, he introduced the 'Wardmaster' system in the hospital huts, whereby combat officers were appointed as Wardmasters responsible for nominal rolls, discipline, cleanliness, meals etc. This enabled the medical orderlies to concentrate on their vital role of caring for the patients. It was a system that undoubtedly raised the survival rates at Tanbaya and contributed greatly to the smooth running of the hospital. The medical staff were assisted by the sole chaplain in the camp, a British officer named Noel Duckworth. Bruce Hunt was awarded an MBE for his work as a PoW. He returned to practise in Perth after the war, and died in 1964 aged 65. Don Wall's book **The Heroes of 'F' Force** *contains numerous personal tributes to Bruce Hunt, and extracts from Hunt's official report on Tanbaya, the Burma Hospital Camp, are at Appendix III.*

Continuing now with Richard's memoir…

At the beginning of April 1943 the Nips told our Camp authorities that the POW population of Changi must be reduced by the transfer of 7,000 men up country, the reason given being that the food situation in Malaya was becoming increasingly difficult (which was true) whilst up country was, in effect, 'a land flowing with milk and honey'. In order to get the required 7,000 men for 'F' Force the Nips offered further 'bait', for example:

1. This would NOT be a working party.
2. We could take 30% unfit men with us who would benefit from the more plentiful and varied food available at our up country destination.
3. Our Concert Party with their instruments (including a piano!) could go with us, plus a generator and gear for electric light.
4. Medical staff and their equipment and medical supplies for 3 months could also be taken.

I never heard which Japanese officer gave these undertakings, but even if he was part of the Nip POW Administration (as opposed to Railway Engineers) he must have known what was in the wind; hopefully he was dealt with accordingly by the Allies after the war.

Shortly before we set off on 'F' Force I received my first Red Cross letter (25 words) from Bobbie in Australia with an extremely attractive photo of herself, which was to prove a great comfort and inspiration in the difficult days which followed. [*This letter had been sent in June 1942, ten months previously.*] It was also a great relief to get confirmation that she had indeed got through to Australia and was a wonderful and, I felt, undeserved surprise as at the time I had had no letters from the UK and I had not been able to get any message out to her in the last days before Singapore fell.

The BSD party for 'F' Force consisted of Dobbie (CO), myself and 16 ORs. We left as part of train Party No.8 from Singapore Station on Sunday 25th April 1943 for our unknown destination up country. Each train party consisted of 600 men, with 27/28 of all ranks travelling in Federated Malay States (FMS) Railway 10-ton all steel goods trucks, measuring 19 feet 3 inches by 7 feet 3 inches. The journey from Singapore to Ban Pong in Thailand took 4 to 5 days; by the time we got to Prai in Province Wellesley (on a level with Penang) we realised that we must be bound for Thailand. This train journey was no tourist excursion and was far from an ideal preparation for what was to come. The steel goods trucks were not exactly spacious for 27/28 men with their kit; at night the trucks were surprisingly cold but in daytime they became like ovens, the sides so hot that one could not lean up against them. Water was rationed at about one pint per man per day for all purposes, and in our de-hydrated state was quite inadequate. Occasionally one came across a co-operative Thai engine driver who allowed us to fill our water bottles from a pressure relief valve on the engine; a great boon, with the added advantage that one knew that the water was completely sterile. One also noted with interest that many of the locomotives on the Thai railway system came from well-known manufacturers in GB.

Other things that I recall from this journey. The first, which left a nasty taste in the mouth, was a party of RAMC Orderlies in our truck who quite blatantly opened, and consumed, large 16 ounce bottles of Marmite which were obviously part of the consignment of Red Cross parcels from the *ASAMA MARU*, and which were intended for the hospitals which we had been promised at our destination. Their behaviour contrasted strongly with that of two Eurasian brothers (named, I think, Rosario and Fernandez) who had elected to go 'into the bag' with the Federated Malay States Volunteer Force (FMSVF) rather than revert to civilian status, which from the point of view of their appearance they could easily have done. These two brothers were, with a very few notable exceptions, streets ahead of the average RAMC Orderly and I remember them with great respect. The other lasting impression from this uncomfortable journey was the beauty and lushness of the Thai countryside as we travelled northwards to Ban Pong, sleek cattle knee-deep in the stubble of the paddy fields surrounding the villages and their temples, themselves surrounded by tall shady trees.

On de-training at Ban Pong we marched three quarters of a mile to a very scruffy and insanitary Transit Camp carrying all our gear, of which there was quite a lot bearing in mind the undertakings given to us by the Nips before leaving Singapore. At the Transit Camp we began to learn what was ahead of us, namely a march north westwards along the Railway trace towards the Three Pagodas Pass (on the Thai-Burma border) in 14 mile stages; the number of stages was not specified. So, many of our possessions had to be ditched, mainly by selling them to the Thais although prices were not good as several parties had gone through ahead of us and it was not a seller's market. After two stages on made-up roads we arrived at the staging camp outside the walls of the small town of Kanchanaburi. This was a bivouac camp, thoroughly uninviting, in which even the kitchens flooded and we were warned that the real march lay ahead of us; all stages to be marched at night to avoid the heat of the midday sun. It was here that I had to ditch more of my load, including a much-prized photograph album which was a record of the whole of my time since leaving home in 1937. [*He never recovered this album, but fortunately had sent the album containing the Shanghai and North Korea photographs (including some that appear in this book) home to his sister Maudie. All his Singapore and Penang photographs were lost.]*

The orders to march by night also brought their snags; from now on we were on unmade-up track and in the dark it was impossible to avoid the roughness of the track, which resulted in many cuts and bruises which later developed into tropical ulcers. Some nights it was so dark that we resorted to tying a piece of white cloth or towel onto our packs so that the man behind could have something to follow. We normally started our march at dusk and would arrive soon after daylight at the next staging camp (bivouac). All too often we were kept on parade all morning, sometimes up to twelve noon and frequently in full sun, to allow stragglers to catch up and for the Nips to get their figures right. At the end of that we had no more than a few hours before we were due to move out again in the evening, and during this time we had to get what food we could (generally rice with a thin vegetable stew) and fit in a few hours rest. Towards the end of the march the monsoon was beginning to break so that our day's 'rest' in these bivouac camps did nothing to refresh us. In the meantime cholera had broken out higher up the line of march and we had to stop at Kinsayok after doing 9 stages. The bivouac at Kinsayok was thoroughly depressing but the great blessing of those two nights was that I was able to rest my feet (which were beginning to be very painful owing to my boots getting full of mud) and to do some much needed repairs on my footwear. After leaving Kinsayok we marched a further seven stages which brought us on 20th May 1943 to our destination, Songkurai No.2 Camp, something over 300 kilometres from Ban Pong and about 9 kilometres short of the Three Pagodas Pass (the Thai-Burma border).

Quite early on in the piece something told me that this march was going to be quite something and I started keeping a diary, purely about the march and only in the barest outline, to serve as a 'skeleton' to write up this story at some time in the future (some 45 years later as it turned out!).

[This is a transcript of that diary, the original of which is now held in the archives of the Imperial War Museum in London. In view of what was to come, it is remarkable that it survived. Punctuation and spelling have been left unchanged from the original.]

SINGAPORE TO SONGKURAI, THAILAND
APRIL – MAY 1943
'F' FORCE, TRAIN No.8

SUNDAY, 25/4/43 Left Singapore 0700 hours with No.8 Train Party for unknown destination up-country. Each train load 600 men with 27/28 all ranks in FMS 10 ton steel CC truck (dimensions 19' 3" x 7' 3").

MONDAY, 26/4/43 Arrived KL [Kuala Lumpur] 0300 hours: collected breakfast – rice and dried fish. Arrived Ipoh 1600 hours for second meal of the day – rice and veg stew. The station platform covered in coal. Able to buy iced coffee – very limited but welcome. Note. A very little buying of fruit from hawkers possible in Malaya but this was stopped on crossing the Thai border.

TUESDAY, 27/4/43 Arrived Prai 0200 hours and collected breakfast. Two hours stop at Padang Besar at 0900 hours for washing (including PT) etc. Water very scarce for rest of the journey – about 1 pint per man per day. 1700 hours arrived Haadyi.

WEDNESDAY, 28/4/43 All day in train, water very short and buying of fruit is forbidden. Rations as usual – breakfast, rice and dried fish, second meal of the day, rice and veg stew. Heat in truck stifling at midday.

THURSDAY, 29/4/43 1100 de-training at Ban Pong and after long delay in the sun marched three-quarters mile to transit camp carrying all equipment and baggage. Transit camp consists of Coolie huts but food good after conditions in train, water still scarce.

FRIDAY, 30/4/43 Preparations for march up-country in 14 mile stages; all but essential equipment abandoned or sold. 'Black Market' fruit and eggs obtainable locally at reasonable rates.

SATURDAY, 1/5/43 1000 hours arrived at first staging camp (Tanara) after long and tiring march having started at 2300 hours the previous night. Well run camp with controlled Canteen and reasonable prices in spite of 'squeeze' to Officials. Lorry arranged to carry baggage for the night.

SUNDAY, 2/5/43 Arrived Kanchanaburi 0830 hours after tiring march although travelling light. Bivouac camp very wet and muddy, food and water scarce. Local 'Black Market' Canteen prices higher than Ban Pong. Fine night – 11 hours sleep.

MONDAY, 3/5/43 Medical inspection in the morning; left on next stage at 2300 hours after long delay. During 36 hours at Kanchanaburi official water issue amounted to about 1 and ½ pints per man. Bivouac camp in semi-swamp in scrubby jungle; cookhouse fires flooded in heavy rain.

TUESDAY, 4/5/43 Arrived at 0915 hours at comfortable camp (Temple Camp) beside river with controlled Canteen. Washed clothes and bodies in river, very welcome and necessary. Arranged ox-cart transport for baggage and worst sickness cases.

WEDNESDAY, 5/5/43 Arrived at next staging camp by river at 0830 hours. March tiring owing to roughness of track after leaving main road shortly after Kanchanaburi – and owing to lack of moon.

THURSDAY, 6/5/43 Rested in bivouac camp one stage only better than Kanchanaburi; water supply and washing arrangements in river reasonable. Food – rice, veg stew and fish; no salt, sugar, tea or meat.

FRIDAY, 7/5/43 Arrived 'Base Camp' at Tarso at 0900 hours after long march of 18 miles, very tiring owing to muddiness of the track. Kept on parade until 1200 hours waiting for stragglers. Moved on same night.

SATURDAY, 8/5/43 Arrived next bivouac camp (Tonchang) at 0730 hours and spent day in bamboo grove – very damp. Food as usual, two meals of rice and veg stew and haversack ration of cold rice. Moved out same night.

SUNDAY, 9/5/43 Arrived 0800 hours at bivouac camp (Hintok), in bamboo for 36 hours rest. Canteen and eggs available at neighbouring working camp. Feet very sore having had to wear shoes owing to boots breaking up.

[Parties like Richard's who were moving 'up the line' were generally accommodated in temporary bivouac camps that were separate from, and less well set up than, the main camps in which those already working on the Railway were based.]

MONDAY, 10/5/43 Rested all day and repaired boots; feet still very sore. Moved out in evening at 2000 hours; good dry march but feet still very sore owing blisters caused by shoes.

TUESDAY, 11/5/43 Arrived at 0800 at bivouac camp (Kinsayok) with very little shade but good river close by. Move at night cancelled for unknown reason.

WEDNESDAY, 12/5/43 Good night's rest; very glad of rest for feet; camp otherwise a bad one. Move again cancelled – no reason given.

[The reason for the stop at Kinsayok was because of a cholera outbreak further up the line.]

THURSDAY, 13/5/43 0830 hours N.9 Train Party arrived and both Parties moved out together at 1930 hours. Feet much improved by two days rest. Good dry march but feet sore again after three stages.

FRIDAY, 14/5/43 Arrived at next staging camp (Brankali) at 0800 hours. Three meals – all rice with very little stew. No local purchase. Camp very strictly run by alleged Imperial Guard Sergeant ('Hitler camp').

Note. No tea or drinking water provided in the staging camps; individuals have to boil their own water or risk chlorinated river water.

SATURDAY, 15/5/43 Arrived Tarkanoon at 0130 hours and had 6 hours sleep by road-side before moving into Bivouac. Well run camp with improved food and fewer restrictions. Moved off 2030 hours after long delay in counting.

SUNDAY, 16/5/43 Arrived at next staging camp (Tameron Pa) 0800 hours after march up hill and down dale but got 4 hours fair sleep on road-side before arrival. Three meals – rice and meat extract soup but very slowly served owing to lack of containers. Rain storm in afternoon.

MONDAY, 17/5/43 Arrived next camp (Konkoita) 0900 after slow and tiring march; no organisation for reception owing to cholera scare, finally bedded down in jungle at 1100 hours. Long walk for all meals. Rain storm in afternoon. Did not move off until 2100 hours.

TUESDAY, 18/5/43 Arrived at 0830 hours at Base Camp (Shimo Nieke) for 18th Div Party after easier march over fair roads. Accommodation in huts without roofs – luxury nevertheless. Improved food rice, fish, towgay [*bean sprouts*] and onion stews. Good night's rest.

WEDNESDAY, 19/5/43 Bombshell at midday – move on tonight. March of 10 miles – cholera scare? Water supply very inadequate – one small muddy stream for 1500 men. Moved off 2400 hours after good meal, with Trains 7 and 9, leaving AIF personnel at a camp (Shimo Sonkurai) 12 kilometres up the road.

THURSDAY, 20/5/43 Slow and tiring march; slow for no apparent reason as road is now much better and shows signs of more care in building. No reception arrangements at final destination; men very crowded in unroofed huts. Officers in luxury – hut with roof! Cook-house do wonders and produce meal by 1400 hours. Very wet night for men.

FRIDAY, 21/5/43 Much rain in night; very hard on men. Cleaning up camp area all day. Some progress made in roofing men's huts. Food fair – rice dried fish and some onions and lentils. Heavy showers all day – monsoon weather.

WEDNESDAY, 2/6/43 Name of this camp is apparently Songkurai [*Actually Naka Songkurai, or Songkurai No.2 – there were three Songkurai camps*] – 300 kilometres from Ban Pong. Deaths from cholera to date 85. Men fit for work – 175 out of approximately 1500. [*Returning to the memoir.*]

Main impressions of the march were:

1. Extreme fatigue, due to stumbling along the rough Railway trace in the dark, and to rations totally inadequate for the energy which we had to expend. This rather than the actual distances we covered, an average stage being 20/25 kilometres. For me, the lesson learnt during long hard days with the Fell Foxhounds in the Lake District that '…you never know what you can do until you damn well have to do it…' kept me going better than most. [*The Fell Foxhound packs in the Lake District in the 1930s hunted entirely on foot across demanding mountainous terrain.*]
2. Footwear (and one's kit generally) were a constant pre-occupation. One's feet became very sore owing to not being able to see where one was going in the dark, but I had it very firmly in my mind that throwing away one's kit (particularly one's boots) was the beginning of the end. It was not easy to bring this home to some of the men who threw their boots and equipment away despite all the warnings; many of them lived (and died) to regret it in the days to come. In September 1945 I was able to 'march out' of captivity

complete with pack, haversack, water bottle and one set of clothing (carefully preserved, by going near naked most of the time), in case at the end there was a chance of slipping away into the bush rather than being massacred in cold blood by the Nips.

3. At one of the early staging camps one bloke in our Train party had with him a beautiful black and white cocker spaniel in very good condition, which had been abandoned at a house in Singapore and which he had recovered. When I asked the owner about the dog, to which he was obviously devoted, he was, rightly, very cagey. I felt sorry for him, for one knew already that to many POWs a dog was simply meat on the hoof. I never saw the dog again although I often wondered what happened to him, and can only hope that if it came to the pinch his Master would have had the courage to knock him on the head himself.

4. Some of the bivouac camps in which we spent the daytime were set in beautiful mountain scenery which reminded me of a Chinese painting. As a lover of mountains I was lucky, in that I really could '…lift up mine eyes unto the hills from whence cometh my help…'

Songkurai No.2 Camp, our final destination, was a depressing place; a half-finished camp with no roofs on some of the huts, and the Monsoon was now starting in earnest. We had at least hoped for a day or two's rest to recover from the march (and also for better rations), but nothing of the sort. Some parties already out working on the Railway and the rest trying to tidy up and finish the Camp in monsoon weather. Rations were a little better for a day or two, but soon started going off because the track alongside the Railway trace, along which all supplies were supposed to come until the Railway went through, became impassable. Also, with our camp being almost the northernmost camp on the line, supplies dwindled to a trickle by the time they got to us. Our first task (necessary for the Nips as well) was therefore to try to make the track passable for vehicles; as a result of this, work on the Railway itself fell behind and the 'Speedo' orders which the Nip Railway Administration had already given became even more strident.

We had already brought cholera with us, having picked it up in the transit Camps on the march. In our weakened state at the end of the march cholera soon got a hold, as did other diseases – dysentery, malaria, beri-beri, tropical ulcers – and within a fortnight of arriving at Songkurai there had already been 85 deaths from cholera alone and only 175 men were classed as fit for work out of a total of some 1600 men who had marched into the camp two weeks before. For the next three months life became one long slog from first light or before until dusk; almost continuous rain, day and night, totally inadequate rations, overflowing latrines (which were in any case only open trenches which merely assisted in the spread of disease), and above all pretty well every tropical disease you could think of. As a result of this, deaths in the camp were at one time running at 25 per day and, a year later, out of the 1600 men who had marched into the camp less than 400 were still alive. These figures were given to me by Major Bruce Hunt AAMC [*Australian Army Medical Corps*] who did a marvellous job on the Medical side of 'F' Force.

[*As a complete contrast, at around this time in June and July 1943, Bobbie, in Melbourne, Australia, was writing to Richard in her 'letters', which she ultimately gave to him in Columbo in October 1945.*]

[*Extract from a letter of Bobbie's to Richard (Dickie)*]

Melbourne
16 June 1943

Dearest,
    Today the News Boys were gleefully (they seem almost to take pleasure in bad news) shouting out that 10 British POWs had been executed in Tokyo. I had to buy a paper to see what details there were, and of course there were none. But it took all the joy out of the day for me. I felt sick and miserable; I don't know where you are and when such items of news come out they frighten me. I should have more faith; because you will come back to me. When I am at the pictures and we are shown the wonderful achievements of the 8th Army I feel intensely proud that I am British, and terribly

sad at the same time thinking of you, and all the others with you, knowing how you would have wanted to be doing your bit instead of being cooped up behind barbed wire. I do pray it will not make you bitter.

There are several Societies organised here by Far Eastern folk with a view to passing around all available news and helping those in distress etc. A circular is issued each month and very interesting they are. The last one stated that there were thousands of British prisoners in Siam and that they had not been permitted to receive or send letters. I wonder if you are with that lot? All these months I have been thinking, although no news has reached me of you, at least you have perhaps had a letter or two (I have sent twelve) from me and that thought was comforting.

God Bless darling, Bobbie

Melbourne
7 July 1943

Hello Dearest,

Darling what strange unnatural lives we are all leading; sometimes I try to picture the lives we would have been leading had Singapore not fallen; you would have come down for your leave last July (I suppose about this time last year) and we would have had lots of fun, probably a sort of repetition of when I was down for Betty's wedding. I was so surprised when you marched into Betty's house (after Penang fell) and kissed me; I don't mean the actual fact of kissing, but it all seemed to imply something more. I did ask you why you didn't give me any indication in your letters and I can't remember getting any satisfactory reply. I wonder why? And now I shall have to wait until after the war. It took me some time to get myself adjusted to the fact that you cared more than a little; and that made me hold back a bit. I didn't expect your proposal on Christmas Eve and was struck a bit dumb; what an ass I was. Had I known what the future was going to bring my answer would have been quite different. However as a bachelor prisoner-of-war you would not feel your responsibilities weigh so heavily as you would as a married man; for that small mercy I should be thankful – you have quite enough to put up with. Dear God, if only I could do something to help you. And there is absolutely nothing I can do, or will be able to do, except write to you one page letters per month and I don't even know whether they reach you. But surely you must feel me near you in thought; I think of you constantly and care so deeply it must form a bridge between us.

Good-night sweetheart, Bobbie

Once the repairs to the access track (laying down parallel lengths of bamboo to form a 'corduroy' surface) were completed, we moved on to work on the Railway itself. This involved pile-driving (including night shifts) for the bridge over the River Kwai Noi adjacent to the camp, and making cuttings and embankments (chungkols and basket-ware hods the only tools) [*a chungkol is a form of spade in which the blade is at right angles to the long handle*]. All this in the pouring monsoon rain which, even for me who prided myself on being psychologically more or less impervious to weather, was a bit too much.

As an officer one was quickly disabused of the idea that under the Geneva Convention officers were not compelled to work, and when in charge of a working party I developed a technique of trying to act as a buffer between our men and the Nips by helping them when they had been allocated a task beyond their capability, and by warning them when they must appear busy and when they could ease off. This worked fairly well and prevented a few bashings until I was rumbled by one Lieutenant Abe, the Engineer in charge of that sector of the Railway, who drew his revolver, cocked it and threatened to shoot me on the spot. As he appeared to mean business I had to be more circumspect thereafter, but the incident was seen by the men of my working party and it was not wasted on them that Lieutenant Abe was a real bad one, not just the usual Bushido attitude, but really vicious as well. Fortunately, Cyril Wild, an outstanding Japanese interpreter, was at Songkurai and quickly took the measure of Lieutenant Abe who was tracked down after the war and stood trial for war crimes – well deserved. In general I did not feel vicious about the Nips, but I certainly did about this one.

Major Cyril Wild was one of the outstanding personalities to emerge from the shambles of the Malayan Campaign and our subsequent 3½ years as 'guests' of the Imperial Japanese Army. He had gone to Japan in pre-war years for the Rising Sun Petroleum Company (in other words 'Shell') and while there had done a 2 year Interpreters Course on which he had learnt not only day-to-day Japanese but also the language of the Imperial Japanese Court. The ability to speak this form of Japanese seemed to give him an immediate psychological ascendency over the ordinary Japanese officers. Notwithstanding this advantage he showed outstanding courage in dealing with the Nips who were under clear orders to get the Railway finished on time – or else! Hence the 'Speedo'. Cyril Wild, to his disgust, had to carry the White Flag at the surrender of Singapore negotiations with the Nips on 15th February 1942, but he also managed to secrete the Union Flag which had been taken to the meeting with General Yamashita. This flag he produced with pride when the Nips surrendered in 1945. Very sadly Cyril Wild was killed in an air crash at Hong Kong in 1946.

The Nips were extremely nervous of cholera and when the outbreak of the disease was confirmed in the camp at Songkurai a so-called cholera 'Isolation Hospital' was set up on the other side of the Railway about a quarter of a mile away from the main camp. This 'hospital', so far as I recall, consisted of a bamboo and attap lean-to and one leaking tent. The 'hospital' was staffed by a Doctor Turner of the Malayan Medical Service (he was a Lieutenant in the FMS Volunteer Force) and two or three orderlies. Food was taken across to them from the main camp and left nearby for collection, so that no direct contact occurred. Medicines for the treatment of cholera were practically non-existent, and in any case many of the men who were sent over to the cholera 'hospital' were beyond treatment by the time they got there. Lieutenant Turner himself caught the disease but treated himself (and recovered) while continuing to treat other patients. He also operated the camp radio set (knowing full well the consequences of doing so if he had been caught); the set was secreted at the cholera 'hospital' as being the one place that the Nips would not dare to go near. I believe that Lieutenant Turner was awarded the MBE after the war; few decorations can have been more richly deserved.

The radio at Songkurai would only be operated rather irregularly owing to the difficulty of charging the batteries, situated as we were miles from any source of electric power and not having any charging engine (impossibly cumbersome in any case). The problem was solved by the courageous co-operation of certain AIF personnel who were driving lorries along the track beside the Railway trace. Originally, a spare battery was 'won' by one of the drivers who complained that the battery on his truck was 'sudah habis' (finished); the Nips produced a replacement and the 'dud' was thrown out, but subsequently recovered. Thereafter batteries needing re-charging were swapped over under cover of spurious breakdowns. The batteries, covered with rice, were carried to and from the trucks by ration parties in the large containers used for cooking the rice. Various diversionary activities were mounted to distract the attention of the Nips while the batteries were being changed. With a covering of rice over it the good battery was then taken over to the cholera 'hospital'. The technical side of the operation and maintenance of the radio was in the charge of a man named James Mudie, a Post Office Engineer serving in the Royal Corps of Signals; to whose courage we all owe a great debt of gratitude. By the time I was transferred to Tanbaya Hospital (on the Burma side of the Three Pagodas Pass) at the beginning of September 1943 the intermittent radio news was enough to let us know that things were going well in the Mediterranean – landings in Sicily and on the mainland of Italy.

[James Mudie recounted how he was very nearly discovered. He normally hid the radio in a latrine, but had a battery, coil of wire and pair of pliers in his hut when the Japanese sprang a surprise search. They were discovered but Mudie got word to Cyril Wild, who simply told

the Japanese that they were part of the hospital equipment and were used to set up lights for emergency operations. Such was Cyril Wild's standing that he was believed, and the hospital was even allowed to keep the equipment.]

It was, incidentally, from the cholera 'hospital' at Songkurai that Jim Bradley (a cholera carrier, but not actually infected) made his escape with his party and after a horrendous journey over a series of precipitous jungle-covered ridges got right across to the River Ye which flows into the Bay of Bengal, only to be recaptured. He tells this remarkable story in his book *Towards the Setting Sun*. The Nip reaction to this escape (by 9 or 10 men of whom 50% did not survive) was remarkably muted with no violent repercussions on the Camp as a whole, although our Camp CO (Lieutenant Colonel Harris) was a very worried man for some time. [*Lieutenant Colonel S.W. Harris, OBE, Royal Artillery, was in fact the CO of 'F' Force, whose headquarters was at Nieke, some eleven kilometres south of Songkurai No.2.*] I suspect that the Nips' relatively muted reaction to the affair was partly due to Cyril Wild's skill in handling them, and to the fact that they themselves felt that the escapees did not stand a 'cat in hell's chance' of surviving in the jungle at the height of the South-West Monsoon.

For me one of the few sources of enjoyment were the elephants which were used in the shifting of the heavy timbers needed for the building of the bridge over the River Kwai Noi adjacent to the Camp. The elephants under the guidance of their Mahouts were quite uncanny in the way that they gauged exactly the right point of balance to shift the heavy timbers; it was a real pleasure in our rather unpleasant existence to watch the elephants at work.

On one occasion when we had got back to camp at the end of the day's work all available men were turned out because a high-ranking Nip officer's car had got irretrievably stuck in the mud a mile or two up the road. A gang of fifty or so emaciated POWs heaving on ropes made no impression whatsoever on the bogged down car, not helped by the fact that the Nip driver persisted in revving his engine and so digging the car even deeper into the mud. Finally a passing elephant was called in to help but the combined efforts of one (half-hearted) elephant and the 50 POWs still made no impression on the bogged down car, until the Mahout waved us all aside because we were obviously putting the elephant off. With a few short words of command from his Mahout the elephant, with loud trumpetings, put his back into the job and the car seemed to literally rise up out of the mud with loud sucking noises and within 30 seconds was on 'dry land'.

One incident I look back on with some amusement was the Nip insistence on 'All men wash tools' before going back to camp in the evening, which some of our men regarded as the last straw on the camel's back. To me the job came quite naturally, as I recalled an occasion at 'Chetwynd' (our house at Birkenhead) 20 odd years before when, at a weekend, we children had borrowed tools out of the Potting Shed and had put them back dirty. Mr Daly, the gardener (and a very good one too) duly found them on Monday morning and reported the matter to my father; all of us children were rightly hauled over the coals in a big way. I have never forgotten the lesson that a good workman always looks after his tools. This was something on which I felt that I could agree with the Nips, if only because with laid-down tasks to be completed in a given time, it was in our interests to have our tools in good condition. (Perhaps the Japanese thinking in such matters may in part account for the competitive edge which they have in industry over their British counterparts.)

In September/October 1943 surviving personnel from Songkurai No.2 and other 'top' camps on the Railway were evacuated to a 'hospital' camp at Tanbaya on the Burma side of the Three Pagodas Pass at Kilometre 383 from Ban Pong. At that time the Railway was not operating except for a few kilometres on the Burma side and the journey was made by truck and on foot. In our by then severely weakened condition this was a real nightmare journey.

I remember being surprised at being transferred to Tanbaya as I did not think I was nearly as unfit as many men at Songkurai. In the event I recall this journey as being an even more severe test that the march from Ban Pong to Songkurai, although not of course as long. One feels, in retrospect, that many of those who died on this journey or at Tanbaya would have stood a better chance of survival if they had not been moved from Songkurai where conditions improved once the Railway came through and the Monsoon dried up. I recall very clearly, and with great sadness, two casualties of this journey. One was Sherwood Connor, at whose wedding in Singapore in June 1940 Bobbie and I had been Bridesmaid and Best Man. Sherwood had very severe tropical ulcers on his legs and died within hours of his arrival at Tanbaya; whether he would have survived I do not know, but the journey did nothing to help him. The other was a very fine young soldier in the Northumberland Fusiliers of whom I had seen quite a lot on various working parties. After we had got over the Pass to the railhead on the Burma side and were waiting to be loaded onto a rail-car, this lad was lying on a stretcher in the sun (which had come out at last) and told me it was his 20th birthday. I tried to cheer him up with hopes of the 'promised land' at Tanbaya but he did not even survive long enough to get that far.

It is worth mentioning here that whilst 'in the bag' I developed great respect for this battalion of the Northumberland Fusiliers. They were a Machine Gun Battalion who had disembarked from the sinking *EMPRESS OF ASIA* in the Singapore Roads (minus all their equipment) on 5th February 1942. Despite this shattering introduction to Malaya their morale as a unit remained of the highest order both during the battle for the Island and as POWs, in contrast to the behaviour of some other units who had had a much easier 'run'.

[*This was 9th battalion Royal Northumberland Fusiliers. They actually landed in Singapore on 5 February 1942 from the French troopship*

Felix Roussel *complete with their equipment (this was the same ship that Richard found, apparently deserted, on 11 February). They fought in the battle for Singapore Island until the surrender on 15 February. They were moved to the Railway in November 1942. From April 1943 the Battalion were used as track-layers, being split up into small groups up and down the line. Survivors eventually returned to Singapore in July 1944, ultimately returning to England in October 1945. The battalion never re-assembled after April 1943.]*

The last camp on the Thai side of the Three Pagodas Pass was called Changavaya and I recall it as the most depressing of all the camps I saw. Morale was bad; there was very little food and deep mud everywhere. There was a long trek from the trucks to the huts, all in the dark and pouring rain, carrying stretcher cases, the kit of the walking sick and our own kit; several trips in all.

I had been looking forward to seeing the Three Pagodas at the summit of the Pass, imagining them to be tall pagodas aspiring heavenwards (as did many of our thoughts), but I was deeply disappointed to find that they were dumpy little structures no more than 8 to 10 feet high as I remember.

We arrived at Tanbaya on the afternoon of that day having covered the last few kilometres in a lorry converted to run on the Railway, which had been completed as far as Rouchi by 'A' Force parties (mainly AIF) working from Thanbyuzayat (Tanbesar), the junction on the existing rail system between Moulmein and Ye. Tanbaya proved to be very far from the 'land flowing with milk and honey' which we had all hoped for; for the first 48 hours after our arrival plain rice was all that was available and feeding was never good throughout our stay at Tanbaya. Supplies to supplement the rice ration, such as eggs, fruit and fish, were just not available in that part of Burma. This was in contrast to the lower camps on the Thai side of the Railway where, at least in the larger and longer established camps, it was possible to supplement the Nip rations by local purchase. The redeeming features of life at Tanbaya were, firstly, that we were not required to do any work on the Railway and, secondly, that the constant rain of the Monsoon had dried up. In fact the weather became dry and sunny, very pleasant in the daytime, but quite cold at night when we had to wear every stitch of clothing we possessed – and frequently that was not enough.

As the dry season advanced the cookhouse, which had been on the edge of the camp, had to be moved to a stream half a mile or more away, as this was the only source of water available in quantity for cooking the rice. Carrying the rice in baskets from the cookhouse to the camp became a major chore, and an onerous one, for convalescent personnel. I still have a scar on my shoulder (my war wound!) from a burn resulting from carrying a basket of hot rice; at the time I did not realise that the hot rice was causing the trouble but thought it was merely the basket cutting into my flesh. Fortunately, Bruce Hunt, the AIF doctor mentioned earlier, thought I was worth expending some of his precious 'M&B' on and my shoulder responded very quickly. [*M&B 693, or sulfapyridine, was one of the first generation of sulphonamide antibiotics.*] Before that, when newly arrived at Tanbaya, Bruce spotted that I had Cardiac Beri-beri and bedded me down until it improved. On these two counts alone I can truly say that I owe my life to him.

The more mobile of us used to combine our rice carrying fatigue with a visit to a small river where there was a pleasant shady pool with a gravel bottom where we could lie and soak. Here our ulcers attracted small 'fingerling' fish which nibbled the rotten flesh around the edges of the ulcers, an unattractive idea at first, but we soon found that it was an effective and relatively painless way of clearing up an ulcer and proved to be effective therapy in the long run.

At Tanbaya tools of any kind were in very short supply, so much so that there was only one hand-saw in the camp. In the morning it was used for cutting up firewood for the cookhouse and for funeral pyres; in the afternoon it was used for carrying out amputations in the 'operating theatre'.

Accommodation at Tanbaya was the usual bamboo and attap hut but, being almost brand new, it was reasonably clean and we managed to keep it that way. In some of the huts the main uprights were saplings from the jungle (rather than bamboo) and, being newly felled, soon 'struck' and put on healthy young green growth. Across the river from our bathing pool was a range of quite steep tree-clad limestone hills about 1500 feet high which provided a welcome change of view from secondary jungle and bamboo. The Nips left us pretty much to our own devices, but I remember a Lieutenant Wakabayashi (always known as 'Rock-a-bye-baby'), a member of the Nip POW Administration who certainly did what he could for us, bearing in mind his limited authority and resources. [*It is believed that Lt Wakabyashi committed suicide following the Japanese surrender in August 1945.*] Another Nip whom I remember as quite a human individual looked like a traditional Italian organ-grinder, and was accordingly christened Antonio (from the old Music Hall song).

In November/December 1943 the Railway line was open right through over the Three Pagodas pass and we were moved by rail from Tanbaya to Kanchanaburi en route back to Singapore. This was a distance of about 340 kilometres (rather over 200 miles) but the journey took 5 days even though at that time there had been no Allied Bombing of the line. Much of the track was still un-ballasted and the rails looked like a pair of snakes worming their way along the rail-bed, so it was not surprising that derailments were frequent. A jack was carried on the train for jacking trucks back onto the line, but if the derailment was too bad the truck was uncoupled and tipped over the edge. Our train started with about 12 trucks but we finished up with only 7, resulting in extreme overcrowding. These trucks were open ones, and behind wood-burning engines we lived in a shower of sparks which in the overcrowded trucks we could not dodge – result, more burns and the ensuing ulcers. The sparks also set fire to one of the wooden bridges over a ravine, resulting in a 36 hour delay while the fire was extinguished (by a chain of buckets carried by sick POWs from the bridge down into the ravine below) and the damaged bridge repaired. One unpleasant feature of this journey was that a few of the sicker men died on the way, but we were not allowed to offload them at the intermediate camps as the nips required that the correct number of 'bods' (dead or alive) must be counted off the train on arrival at Kanchanaburi.

For me one pleasant but very brief reunion (from a moving train!) was to see Claude Healey (2/3 Motor Transport Company AIF) from Penang days; he was by now a member of a working party from A Force doing maintenance work on the Railway. As the train was moving very slowly on a gradient we had a chat lasting some two or three minutes. [*Captain Claude Healey AIF commanded 2/3 Reserve Motor Transport Company AIF in Penang and Singapore. He survived the war to return to Sydney.*]

We stayed a week or 10 days at Kanchanaburi awaiting onward transport to Singapore. The camp here was considerably improved since we passed through at the end of April 1943 in that it was no longer a bivouac camp. We were accommodated in the usual bamboo and attap huts and the food was somewhat better, but still not good enough to save the lives of some of our number from 'F' Force who had come down from the 'top' camps. It was here that I heard that my photograph album (ditched as the last non-essential before setting off on our march to the Three Pagodas Pass area) had been seen sculling around the camp. Sadly I was never able to track it down as it would have been quite a prize to bring back to Bobbie when I did meet her again, containing as it did the photographs of the Sherwood Connor/Betty Gordon wedding in June 1940 where Bobbie and I had first met.

I have a vivid recollection of one particularly sad incident in Kanchanaburi on the return trip, namely a meeting with Johnnie Walters of the Hong Kong and Shanghai Bank whom I knew in Penang in 1940/41, a very good bloke with a lovely blonde Canadian wife. Johnnie, a Private in the SSVF (Singapore Straits Volunteer Force), approached me wanting to earn a little extra money by darning socks for the purchase of additional vitamins; this was an offer I did not accept, instead 'loaning' him 10 Ticuls. [*Thai currency.*] Poor Johnnie was dead within a matter of days from beri-beri, although at the time I saw him he did not look as bad as some. I felt, and still feel, very sad about this; such a contrast to the happy days in Penang, but above all he was someone who deserved to survive because he was always willing to do the most menial tasks to help himself rather than just sitting back and bemoaning his luck.

The journey back to Singapore was still in the steel goods wagons but a good deal more relaxed than the journey north as we were not nearly so crowded. The Nip guards were not so aggressive; food and water was more plentiful and we were able to buy fruit etc more freely from the Thais and Malays alongside the line.

Chapter Five

Prisoner of War – Changi and Freedom December 1943 to October 1945

After his arrival back in Changi in late December 1943, Richard spent some time convalescing. He recounts the fall-out from the raid on Japanese shipping in Singapore Roads mounted by an SOE force based in Australia, which impacted particularly on the civilian internees housed in Changi Jail.

This raid, Operation Jaywick, was a clandestine attack on Japanese shipping in Singapore Harbour conducted on 26 September 1943 by commandos based in Australia. The raid was the brainchild of an SOE operative, Captain (later Lieutenant Colonel) Ivan Lyon, and a 61-year-old Australian civilian, Bill Reynolds. The plan was to travel to the vicinity of Singapore Harbour in a disguised Asian fishing boat, then use collapsible canoes (folboats) to enter the harbour and attach limpet mines to Japanese ships. Reynolds had a 70 foot Japanese fishing boat, the Kofuku Maru, in which he had evacuated refugees from Singapore before it fell. Lyon renamed the vessel Krait, after a small but deadly Asian snake. Personnel for the raid comprised 3 British and 11 Australians. They left Exmouth Gulf, in north-west Australia, on 2 September 1943. Krait hid in the Rhio Archipelago and six of her crew paddled their folboats fifty kilometres into Singapore Harbour where, on 26 September, they attached limpet mines which sank or damaged six merchant ships, totalling around 25,600 tons. They successfully returned to the Krait, and arrived back safely in Exmouth Gulf on 19 October 1943.

A subsequent, more ambitious operation (Operation Rimau) comprising twenty-three men, was mounted from the submarine HMS Porpoise in September 1944, led once again by Ivan Lyon. The raiders were discovered by the Japanese and, in a series of running battles with the Japanese, Ivan Lyon and 12 of the party were killed. The remaining 11 were captured; one died of malaria and the remaining 10 were executed by the Japanese on 7 July 1945, less than a month before the Japanese surrender.

At the time of Richard's return from the Burma Railway, conditions in the Changi complex were comparatively good. However, during 1945 food started to become scarce as the Allied submarine and air campaign took an increasing toll of the Japanese merchant fleet, severely restricting their ability to move oil, food and other resources.

In fact, the Japanese defeat caught the Japanese Command in Singapore by surprise, and many were unwilling to surrender. General Itagaki initially baulked at the order to surrender; he ordered his troops to resist when the Allies arrived, and there was indeed a secret plan to massacre all Allied PoWs on the Island. However, on 18 August Itagaki flew to Saigon in a specially marked aircraft (painted white with green crosses) to confer with his superior, Field Marshal Count Terauchi. Terauchi prevailed over Itagaki who subsequently sent a signal surrendering his command to Admiral Mountbatten, Supreme Allied Commander South East Asia. The Allied fleet arrived in Singapore on 4 September, and the formal Japanese surrender of the 77,000 troops in Singapore and 26,000 in Malaya was signed on board HMS Sussex in Singapore Harbour on 12 September 1945. The evacuation of Allied prisoners of war to Australia and India started shortly afterwards.

The period between the official Japanese surrender on 15 August 1945 and the arrival of the Allied Fleet at Singapore on 4 September 1945 was one of great uncertainty for the prisoners of war, because no-one was really sure how the Japanese were going to behave and there remained a very real fear that they might attempt to massacre the prisoners. This gradually receded once it became known that General Itagaki had indicated on 20 August to Admiral Mountbatten his willingness to abide by the Emperor's decision. The first Allied officer to enter Changi was a Canadian SOE officer, Lieutenant Colonel Bob Stewart.

Cyril Wild wrote an article, 'Expedition to Singkep', that was published (posthumously) in Blackwood's Magazine in October 1946. This principally describes his actions as War Crimes Liaison Officer to track down the Japanese Kempeitai responsible for the execution of the ten surviving Operation Rimau personnel in July 1945, and the deaths of fifteen civilian internees arrested during the 'Double Tenth' purge in the wake of the Operation Jaywick attack on Singapore. However, in his article he also describes the period between the Japanese surrender and the arrival of Allied occupying troops.

'The officer who relieved us was Lieutenant Colonel Bob Stewart of the Canadian Army, formerly of the Vancouver Police. He had parachuted some weeks before into Johore from India to join the Chinese guerrillas. One day he arrived in Changi Camp in a Chevrolet roadster commandeered from a Japanese general in Johore Bahru. Even the Japanese were startled at the contrast between his magnificent physique and our somewhat attenuated frames. With Stewart I spent a happy week touring the Island, with a Union Jack flying on the roadster. We visited the Civilian Internment Camp at Sime Road, and all the camps of the loyal Indian prisoners of war. Later, Major Cooper, an aerodrome engineer, arrived from the Cocos Islands in a Mosquito. With him, as his interpreter, I visited all the aerodromes on the Island, to measure them up and see that the Japs had taken the propellers off their planes. While General Itagaki still kept up his boasting that he would fight for Malaya and Singapore, we saw his men piling their arms and shuffling northwards across the Causeway in their thousands.

'So far the local population had dared do no more than give surreptitious V-for-victory and thumbs-up signs as our car with the Union Jack sped past. But today, as we returned from Tengah Aerodrome, we could scarcely drive through the cheering crowds in Singapore. And the cheering was loudest wherever disconsolate Japanese sentries were still standing beside the road. The explanation came as we reached Keppel Harbour and I saw the first flight of 5th Indian Division, in their unfamiliar jungle-green, advancing with fixed bayonets past the godowns.'

Returning for the final time to Richard's memoir, and his and Bobbie's letters...

We arrived back at Changi shortly before Christmas 1943 and received a warm and heartening 'welcome home' from the now much reduced residents of Changi. Some had been kept back because they had wives in the Civilian Internment Camp and some because they were unfit in one way or another. A few 'F' Force parties had got back before us and so the Changi residents had for the first time got direct first-hand accounts of conditions on the Railway and in 'F' Force in particular. The residents were duly impressed and, out of the resources available, went out of their way to make things as good as possible for us. In particular I received quite a batch of letters of the 24-word Red Cross variety from Bobbie, which had been fortunately kept back for us in Singapore rather than being sent on chasing us up the Railway. These letters were indeed heartening and re-assuring as I had not been able to send anything out to her.

Among the things we heard of on getting back to Changi was that in October 1943 the Nips had, without warning, turned The Jail (where the Civilians were still interned) inside out and found various 'incriminating' documents namely pipe dreams for the re-construction of post-war Malaya, but highly suspicious to the Nips. As a result a considerable number (more than 40) of the Civilian Internees were taken to the Kempeitai HQ in the YMCA Building in Singapore and 'given the works' in an attempt to obtain confessions, as a result of which 15 of them died. [*The Kempeitai was the military police arm of the Japanese army. It was both a conventional military police organisation and a secret police force.*]

This raid by the Kempeitai was sparked off by the sinking of (or serious damage to) some 50,000 tons of shipping in Singapore Harbour. The Nips were convinced that this was an 'inside job', carried out by local Chinese with the backing of the Civilian Internees in Changi Jail, particularly as these events took place around 10th October – the 'Double Tenth', a date of particular significance to the Chinese. In fact it was a highly successful sabotage raid organised by the SOE in Australia, led and executed by Ivan Lyon in a captured Japanese Motor Fishing Vessel (MFV) renamed KRAIT. Lyon and his party got into Singapore Harbour (in canoes for the final stretch), attached limpet mines to selected targets and then returned to the KRAIT which was lurking in the Rhio Archipelago, before making their escape back to Australia. The Nips, at the time, had no idea what had hit them, hence the Kempeitai raid on the Changi jail. When Ivan Lyon got back to Melbourne after the JAYWICK operation, as this raid was known, Bobbie was working as secretary to the Head of the SOE Mission in Melbourne, and to her fell the task of typing up Ivan Lyon's official report on JAYWICK (a highly confidential document) – a measure of the high regard in which Bobbie was held.

At the time of our return from 'F' Force life in Changi was still quite civilised. There were lectures, a football league (soon to be stopped as our diet did not warrant exercise of this kind) and even a 'Café' (run by POWs) where of an evening one could sit out in the open and have a cup of 'coffee' (burnt rice!) and a bun (a concoction of rice polishings and tapioca flour). News bulletins (verbal) were also available (very welcome as they had been few and far between up at Tanbaya). Under this regime I put on weight (of the 'watery' rice variety) and reached well over 10 stone, the heaviest I have ever been in my life! We were accommodated in semi-permanent huts in Birdwood Camp adjacent to the 15 inch gun battery on the opposite side of the main road to Changi Village from Selarang Barracks. Here limited supplies of Guy le Mesurier's 'gin' were still available (also fresh limes) so for a limited few weeks we were still able to have our Sunday morning 'gimlet'.

This relatively civilised existence did not, however, last long because in April/May 1944 the Civilian Internees, who had been in the Jail at Changi, were moved to Sime Road Camp (near the Royal Singapore Golf Club) and we, the POWs, were moved into the Jail and the attap huts and coolie lines adjoining it. The Nips had by then ordained that Officers and ORs should be segregated. The Officers went into the attap huts and coolie lines (not bad accommodation by our 'F' Force standards), and the ORs were put in the Jail itself – solid concrete and very crowded. A row of houses outside the Jail which had been the European Warders Quarters became the Camp Hospital. We did have electric light and running water; both a great boon. The Camp Concert Party had been kept intact and with the resources available (stage lighting, scenery and one or two very able and convincing female impersonators) they put on some very impressive shows, which attracted numbers of Japanese officers – sitting in the 'front row of the stalls'!

At one stage, either shortly before or shortly after moving into the Jail, I had a recurrence of Malaria and/or Dysentery and was moved to a temporary 'hospital' in hutted accommodation on Sembawang Rubber Estate – only a short stay, but I remember two things very clearly. Firstly there was a Camp Concert Party whose instruments seemed to be mainly of the percussion variety. The Concert Party gave their performances on the far side of a range of brick-built Rubber Estate buildings with the result that one heard a lot of percussion but very little music. I sometimes think that my later aversion to 'Pop' music dates from that time. Secondly Bruce Hunt was himself a patient at Sembawang, and was busily working on casualty figures for 'F' Force; he told me that of the 1,600 men who had marched into Songkurai No.2 a year ago, only 400 were still alive. This figure for casualties is well above the average for 'F' Force as a whole, let alone for all POWs working on the Railway, but Bruce assured me that he was satisfied that his figures for Songkurai No.2 were correct. [*See also Cyril Wild's narrative report at Appendix I, and Lieutenant Colonel Dillon's report to the IJA at Appendix II.*]

By the time we moved into the Jail the Nips were beginning to demand more and more working parties, initially for the air-strip which they were building that ran parallel to the coast up towards Changi Point, and later for excavating tunnels and bunkers in various parts of the Island for use in last-ditch stands which they were putting up in all parts of the Pacific. Having no wish, after my experience with 'F' Force, to get involved in working parties of this kind I volunteered, before the pressure really came on, for a job on the Camp Gardens. At this job one could work at one's own speed; it was a pleasant way of filling in the day in the Malayan sunshine, and one felt that one was doing something positive for the POW community. The Camp gardens were adjacent to the Jail Sewage Farm, the sludge from which was dug out and used to fertilise our crops. We were assured by our own Medical authorities that the sludge treated in this way was innocuous, which I think was basically correct. Certainly there was no undue smell from it such as one got from the untreated night soil collected from Chinese areas of Singapore city. Our other main fertiliser was urine collected from the whole camp and used in diluted form to encourage the growth of green vegetables. These measures undoubtedly produced remarkable crops from very unpromising soil, and at their peak were sufficient to provide 4 to 6 ounces of vegetables per man per day for the whole camp. This was more significant as a means of balancing our rather thin rice diet, than as any actual increase in bulk. As time went on the Nip issue of rations steadily decreased and the foodstuffs we grew ourselves became more and more important. The Nips laid down ration scales in descending order for 'Fit Men', 'Light Duty' and 'Sick', but we tried to level it out more equitably for all personnel. Speaking from memory, the above categories provided for 2,500, 2,000 and 1,600 calories per day per man; this compares with the 4,000 calories per day considered reasonable for a man doing heavy physical labour, such as building an aerodrome! Towards the end the Nips were not even able to keep ration scales up to the levels which they had themselves prescribed, and I believe by that time that the camp as a whole was only getting 1,600 calories per man per day. Certainly one could see people getting steadily thinner and thinner; many of us were living examples of a man being 'on the bones of his arse'. To some extent rations for the whole Camp were supplemented by purchases through the Canteen; such purchases laid emphasis on vitamin-rich foods such as pea nuts, rice polishings etc, and were financed by deductions from Officers' pay. My pay as a Captain totalled $122.50 per month (in 'Banana money') made up as follows:

$ 27.00	Deducted by the IJA for Food and Accommodation!
$ 45.50	Banked by the IJA for my benefit after the war.
$ 20.00	Contributed to Canteen funds.
$ 30.00	Received by me.
$122.50	Total

One came to regard the first two items, deductions by the Imperial Japanese Army, with a certain wry humour.

Food in 1944/45 did become an increasing pre-occupation, but there were many activities which helped to keep us going as a community, such as:

Wood Parties. These were sent to any remaining areas of rubber on the Island to collect firewood for the Cookhouses.

Borehole Digging (Latrines). This was a means of keeping the sanitation problem under control.

Tailors Shop. The main purpose was to make up clothes out of any material available for the sick, and for those with literally nothing. Mostly we did our own repairs ourselves, and did without clothes as far as possible, wearing G-strings only. Apart from one complete outfit which I kept on one side for the possible 'final emergency' I had one much repaired pair of shorts which had none of the original cloth left in them. I was very proud of my handiwork, but decided against taking it out with me to show Bobbie, firstly because they were probably full of 'steam tugs' [*bugs*] and lice, and secondly because I thought it might cause Bobbie to form too high an opinion of my tailoring skill!

Boot Repair Shop. This undertook the very necessary work of repairing or improvising footwear for the men who had to go out on working parties.

Vitamin Factory. This included the making of Toddy [*A drink made from the sweetish sap yielded by young toddy palm flower stalks when cut.*] which was high in Vitamin B content and was issued to serious Beri-beri patients.

Artificial Limb Factory. For men who had had limbs amputated.

Soap and Tooth Powder Shop. Made from local materials.

Book-binding Shop. To keep the Camp's stock of books going.

Pottery Shop. To make eating utensils and Clay Pipes (people even managed to devise smoking materials of a sort).

Brush Factory. Making brushes from coconut husks.

Medical. Manufacture, among other things, of 'Milk of Magnesia' and Stramonium for Asthma patients. [*Stramonium is a homeopathic/Chinese remedy for asthma made from the dried leaves and flowering/fruiting tops of Datura Stramonium.*]

Lectures and Language Classes. On any subject under the sun.

<u>Camp Gardens</u>. In addition to the 'official' vegetable gardens in which I worked, every spare space outside the huts was cultivated. Tomatoes were a favourite crop as plenty of seeds were found in the sludge from the Sewage Farm.

In terms of keeping up morale, by far the most important Camp interest was 'news'. From the time we moved into the Jail area, the News Service functioned with great efficiency and very few interruptions, a great tribute to those running the Service (whose names I never knew, nor the mechanics of how they obtained their information; the less one knew about these things the better). We certainly knew about D-Day in Europe within 48 hours of it happening, and this sort of standard was maintained right through to VE Day, and to the dropping of the Atomic Bombs on Hiroshima and Nagasaki. The system for news distribution was that a representative of each hut went to a given place each day (but time and place varied), and there the news was passed on verbally. The hut representative went back to the hut and there passed on the news to selected individuals from different sections of the hut. I was fortunate in being co-opted as the representative for our hut and so got the news that much closer to the horse's mouth. This was important as it was extraordinary how some news items became distorted in course of transmission; all news had to be passed on by word of mouth and any taking of written notes was strictly 'verboten'. I enjoyed this small duty greatly as it was very good mental exercise and, as I had a reasonable knowledge of the geography of Europe, and of Germany in particular, it was that much easier to recognise the place names and so get a better idea of what was happening, which I could then pass on to my listeners. I knew that there were certain risks involved, but we were extremely careful (eg sentries posted to give warning if there were any Nips around) and we were not troubled by the fashionable modern phenomena of 'leaks' and 'moles'. I do not know if the Nips suspected what was going on, but, as far as I know, they never got any leads.

[Around this time, on 28 December 1944, Richard wrote to Bobbie. The envelope is addressed thus.]

In the event of my death only to be forwarded to:
   Miss E.G. Couper Patrick
   c/o Commercial Bank of Sydney, 251 Collins Street, Melbourne, Australia

Changi P.O.W. Camp
28.12.44

Bobbie Darling,

I hope it will never be necessary for this letter to be sent to you, for I am putting it away with my private papers – such as they are now – and it will only be sent on to you in the event of anything happening to me. Although you will not have heard anything from me since I became a prisoner of war, I do want you to know that the memory of you has been a very lively one all the time. As you must have realised long since our chances of corresponding at all with our kith and kin have been very limited; to be exact three 24-word post cards in just under three years. I sent them all home to my sister-in-law in England because I wanted them to know for certain that I was all right; it was not until after the third one had been sent that I got a letter from home acknowledging the first one. I asked them at home to let you know I was safe and sound and I do hope that something has got through to you; in any case, the next card shall go to you direct Bobbie.

Your letters to me have come through wonderfully well, even if somewhat slowly – average time in transit 12 months – but I now have a practically complete series from you up to March 1944. It is wonderfully cheering to get your letters, old as they are by the time they get here. Above all I value the photos which you have sent from time to time; they are worth such a hell of a lot to me now that you too are limited in the amount you can write. I did have two photos of you cut out of groups at Sherwood's wedding, but they got completely ruined by rain and sweat during our jaunt up-country to Burma and Siam, and so you can imagine what a joy it has been to get up-to-date pictures to replace them. To date I have got six of them and each one seems to be better than the one before.

Darling Bobbie, I am so very sorry to hear the news about your father; I know these things are bound to happen sooner or later, but somehow it seems to me to be an undeserved end to a useful life to die in a wartime internment camp. [*Bobbie's father, Dr Harry Couper Patrick, died in Shanghai on 16 August 1942 having been ill for some months, during which time he was able to remain in his flat with his wife, Ida. After the Japanese takeover of the International Settlement in December 1941 they had remained in Shanghai, and he had been allowed to continue with his work as the Medical Superintendent of the Shanghai General Hospital and surgeon to the Lester Chinese Hospital. Ida remained in Shanghai after his death, eventually being repatriated to Sydney in late 1945, where she lived until her death in 1960.*]

By the time this letter reaches you – which I hope will never be necessary – you will probably have heard of Sherwood's death in Burma. It would make a long story if I were to tell you all that he went through, but I can only say here that he showed just that patient courage and cheerfulness under really frightful conditions which one would expect of him. Briefly, both he and I were in a batch of 7,000 prisoners sent up to Thailand to build a railway into Burma, of which 3,100 had died within a year. Of the 1,600 men who originally arrived in our working camp – one of the worst of the whole lot – 1,200 had died within a year. I am writing this to you in order that you may pass on to Betty such of it as you think fit. Personally, I think she should know the full facts, as without them she can never fully realise the very high order of courage shown by her husband; she can also bring her son up to think of the father he will never see as a very brave man.

For myself, apart from our personally conducted tour of Burma and Thailand, I have not had a bad time at all; I am now very fit, all things being considered, and am only writing this on the outside chance that I am never able to tell you these things in person. As you may imagine, our main trouble now is boredom and impatience, but I am getting over them pretty well by keeping myself busy with gardening and studies of various kinds. God bless you darling Bobbie, for all your kindness and devotion.

My very best love to you, dear heart, Dickie.

Prisoner of War – Changi and Freedom Dec. 1943 to Oct. 1945   121

On 5 November 1944 we had a wonderful 'Guy Fawkes Day' surprise when a biggish formation of B29s flew over, bombing the Naval Base, apparently quite unaffected by anti-aircraft fire and Nip fighters. These were the first Allied planes we had seen since the surrender in February 1942 and the sight of them gave us a tremendous lift. These raids continued at intervals until early in 1945, and then ceased completely so that we felt rather let down. We did not see any more Allied planes until quite near the end when the Australians had got into Borneo and were able to operate long-range Lockheed Lightnings from there; the Nips seemed to have virtually nothing to put up against them. I did see a solitary 'Zero' get up from the new Changi Airfield to challenge the Lightnings once, but he was set upon very smartly by about five Lightnings and shot down; I almost felt sorry for him. In later years I learnt that the B29s had been operating from airfields in 'Free' China, a remarkable performance in that all their supplies of fuel, bombs etc had had to be flown in over 'the Hump'. [*'The Hump' was the name given to the eastern end of the Himalayan Mountains, over which Allied pilots flew military transport aircraft from India to China to resupply Chiang Kai-Shek's forces in southern China and units of the US Army Air Force based in China. The 'India-China Ferry' started in April 1942 and continued right through to the end of the war, transporting some 650,000 tons of materiel, at great cost in men and aircraft. In all some 594 aircraft and 1,660 personnel were lost.*] Eventually the Nips decided that enough was enough and staged a land offensive in the south-western provinces of China, which Chiang Kai-Shek's troops had not been able to stop. As a result the Americans had had to withdraw from their airfields in that part of China and the B29s had been transferred to the Pacific to re-inforce the assault on Japan itself.

In 1945 'The News' about the closing months of the war became almost routine. We knew of the surrender of Germany and VE Day in Europe; of the remarkable achievements of General Slim and his 14th Army in driving right down through Burma to Rangoon;

of the increasing Allied (mainly American) pressure on Japan itself, including the 'Fire Raids' on Japanese cities, and the occupation, after bitter fighting, of the outlying Japanese 'Home Islands' (Okinawa and Iwo Jima). We also knew that the invasion of Malaya by our forces was only a matter of time and some of us wondered if the Nips would bump us all off in cold blood. I had my own plan, which I did not discuss with anyone, of keeping a small stock of non-perishable rations and one complete set of carefully husbanded clothing (including boots) aside and, hopefully, slipping quietly through the wire one dark night and lying low until I could contact friendly forces.

In the meantime life in Changi went on relatively peacefully and, having made my plan (such as it was) for evading a massacre by the Nips, I concentrated on daily living – work in the camp gardens and the daily 'News' sessions. This was interrupted by odd spells in Hospital (the former European Warders' quarters just outside the Jail) with recurrences of Malaria and Dysentery; also an attack of Renal Colic which, in terms of pain, was the worst thing I have ever experienced. During one Hospital spell one of my fellow patients was a very charming and intelligent Italian Naval Commander who, having been an enemy up to September 1943, finished up as a fellow POW with us in Changi. He had been in command of an Italian submarine operating in the Indian Ocean, which happened to be in Penang at the time of the Italian surrender. The submarine was promptly arrested by the Nips and the ship's company was given the choice of continuing to fight on the side of the Axis or surrendering and becoming POWs. Most of the ship's company felt that they had had enough of the war and surrendered, although I gather that the more ardent Fascists among them were singularly unimpressed.

Towards the end our rations became increasingly meagre and, as a means of supplementing them by local purchase on the Black Market, I decided to flog my wrist watch which, at some peril from time to time, I had carefully husbanded as a form of final 'currency reserve' for just such an emergency as was now arising. I entrusted it to a brother Officer who was on daily working parties in Singapore and claimed to have reliable contacts with the Chinese. As time went on and nothing happened I started chasing this Officer and was fobbed off, rather sheepishly I thought, with excuses that he had lost touch with his Chinese contact. Eventually I had to write my wrist watch off, but I always thought that the gent in question had 'flogged' it for his own purposes. What irked me more than anything about this incident was that this was the watch which I had bought at Gammeters on Collyer Quay on 30 January 1942 when Bobbie was with me, and just minutes before we said 'Good-bye'. So far as I was concerned that watch had a very special significance, and I was only disposing of it as a last resort.

Another incident connected with our farewell in Singapore on 30 January 1942, which was also to leave a nasty taste in my mouth, concerned the Chinese Silver Dollar which Bobbie gave me as a 'Good Luck' talisman. This Silver Dollar I guarded, as it were with my life, all through my 3½ years in captivity ('F' Force and all) and showed it with pride to Bobbie on arrival in Colombo on 24 October 1945, only to have it pinched off my bedside table in the Officer's 'dormitory' in the Galle Face Hotel in which I was accommodated. I have always suspected that the culprit was one of my brother officers; but at least it had done its job by then.

In August 1945 news came through of the dropping of the Atomic Bombs on Hiroshima and Nagasaki and of the opening of negotiations for the unconditional Japanese surrender. This was agreed by the Emperor for 15/16 August, about a week after the dropping of the Bomb on Nagasaki. At that time however there was no indication from the local Nips in Singapore that they knew about, or accepted, the surrender. So, while we knew that the outside world was celebrating VJ Day, we still had to keep our heads down and pretend that nothing had happened, a pity because 16 August was my birthday and I would dearly have loved to celebrate. Working parties continued to go out to work on the

Airfield but, to their great credit, none of them ever let on to the Nips by undue cockiness that they knew of the surrender. This was important, because when Allied planes came over on or about 20 August the Nips let fly at them with everything they had, and matters were clearly at a very delicate stage. We learned that the Nip commander, General Itagaki, had categorically refused to accept the Surrender (in suspicion that it was all a trick on the part of the Allies) until he had received a direct assurance from a personal representative of the Emperor whom he knew and would trust. The Emperor's personal representative, Prince Terauchi, was flown down to Singapore in a specially marked aircraft painted white with green crosses; I remember seeing it when it flew over Changi.

During this rather tense period (I think before the formal signing of the surrender document) one of our planes, a Mosquito on a reconnaissance flight from the Cocos Islands, had developed engine trouble near Singapore and had, very bravely, decided to take a chance and land at Kallang to try to get some help. Fortunately the Nips at Kallang had by then realised that the game was up and were very co-operative. They enquired at Changi whether we had any RAF Mechanics amongst us, which we had, and they were swiftly whisked off to Kallang where they were able to diagnose and rectify the fault. The next day, the Mosquito took off and, before setting course for the Cocos Islands, did a couple of flat out low level passes over the Jail – a terrific thrill for us who had never seen a Mosquito before, an entirely new generation of aircraft for us.

Shortly after this, ie during the last days of August, a Liberator flew over dropping, not the 'goodies' we all hoped for, but leaflets urging us to stay put in the Camp rather than venture into the world outside – probably good advice, but a bit disappointing. Most of the leaflets fell into the latrine area where, paper being in very short supply, they were quickly used up. I have often regretted that I did not pocket just one leaflet, which I could easily have done, to retain as a little bit of history. We need not however have worried

Prisoner of War – Changi and Freedom Dec. 1943 to Oct. 1945   125

about the lack of 'goodies' because the Nips now started releasing quantities of Red Cross stores which they had been sitting on, probably for their own use against the day when Singapore might come under siege by the Allies. It was at this time that the Nips made an issue of Nipponese Army blankets, a bit superfluous in the Singapore climate, but I kept mine on principle as we got so few free issues from the Nips. I still have it (March 1988) in use as insulation for the water tank in my greenhouse.

In the last days before the Surrender I got a severe recurrence of Malaria (MT++++ (four pluses)), which is the heaviest infection of the malignant form of Malaria, and of which our Medical Authorities took a rather serious view. They therefore sent along a couple of Orderlies with a stretcher to cart me off to Hospital. As the attack of Malaria did not feel to me any more severe than usual, and as I felt far from being a stretcher case, I told the Orderlies that I would walk to Hospital but that they could carry my kit, such as it was, on the stretcher; this arrangement was accepted, under protest, and honour was satisfied. I got over this attack quite normally, and I have often wondered whether the Lab got my slide muddled up with that of some other unfortunate individual who did indeed have Malaria MT++++. Shortly after the Surrender I had to go back into Hospital with another attack of dysentery and, although I did not feel too bad, I was kept in.

It was whilst there in the very early days of September that I got a message that I was required in one of the nearby Warders' Quarters by a Lieutenant Colonel Stewart, whom I had never heard of. He turned out to be one of the operatives with Force 136 [*the Malayan country section of SOE*] who had been parachuted into the jungle in Johore, and who had now emerged and set up his office with a Radio Operator in one of the Warders' Quarters. Having identified myself, I was given a message from 'Miss Patrick' for Captain Laird RASC to say that she was in Colombo with Force 136. As there was obviously very heavy traffic on this one radio link, I was informed very firmly that all I could do was to confirm that I was indeed the Captain Laird after whom Miss Patrick was enquiring and that I was in Changi and alive and kicking. All the letters which I had up till then received (having been in transit for 6 to 9 months) gave her address as c/o her Bank in Australia, and I had been firmly under the impression that she was still there. I had therefore after the Nip surrender already begun to debate whether I should get myself repatriated to UK or Australia. Bobbie's message, apart from the surprise and excitement of being in touch with her, however tenuously, so early after the surrender, partly solved the problem of repatriation, as Colombo was at least on the way to the UK. I learned later that Bobbie's boss in Colombo (John Pickering of Guthrie's – Head of the Malayan Country Section of Force 136) had, off his own bat, offered to let her send a message via the Force 136 radio network to somebody 'Special' who might be in Changi. This she did, an act of great faith on her part as she did not know where I was (or even if I was still alive) and the odds against me being in Changi were considerable.

Colonel Stewart was a Canadian (the first person I had met from the outside world), very business-like in his jungle-green uniform and lace up leech-proof boots. Above all I was impressed by how strong and fit he and his Radio Operator both looked in comparison to the walking skeletons which we had all become. 'Force 136' was also a new one on me, as were so many of the organisations which had sprung up while we were out of circulation. There seemed to be so much to catch up on.

A few days later I was told that I was to be evacuated from Singapore on a Hospital Ship, not that I really felt that I had earned Hospital Ship treatment. Possibly the rather lurid medical history of 'F' Force personnel caused our Medical Authorities to err on the side of caution. And so, on the 9 or 10 of September we were transferred to Keppel harbour and embarked on the *AMARAPOORA*, an ex-Henderson Line boat of 8,000 tons built in 1920 and now converted for use as a Hospital Ship carrying 600 patients, accommodated in long 'wards' in double-decker bunks.

I have two recollections of the *AMARAPOORA* before we sailed. The first was how beautiful Singapore Harbour looked; blue sea and sky with white woolly clouds overhead, and the vivid green of Blakang Mati and the islands beyond. The second memory is of the visit to the ship by Lady Louis Mountbatten, in her capacity as a 'big shot' in St John's Ambulance Brigade. She went round the wards and spoke to every one of the 600 patients, a marvellous feat of endurance in the crowded wards of this rather old ship lying alongside the wharf in the full tropical heat with only fans to stir the air around – no nonsense like air-conditioning! One could see that she was feeling the strain, but this made one's admiration for her all the greater, having hitherto thought of her as just a very upper crust 'Society Lady'.

In our impatience to be 'going places' the trip across the Indian Ocean in the *AMARAPOORA* seemed incredibly slow and, having left Singapore on 9th or 10th September, we did not arrive at Madras until 19th September. In fairness to the *AMARAPOORA* we should have realised that she was quite an old ship (built 25 years ago) and a hard used one, and also that she had to steer a careful course to avoid minefields, which at that stage had not been cleared. At first the Authorities were very cagey about where we might be going, but eventually hinted that it <u>might</u> be Madras and then on to Bangalore (I had hoped it would be Colombo). It was not until the day before we landed that Bangalore via Madras was confirmed as our destination.

[*Telegram from Richard to Bobbie 20th September 1945.*]
   To: *Miss E G COUPER PATRICK, HQ FORCE 136 SEAC COLOMBO.*
   ALL WELL GOING HOSPITAL BANGALORE LOVE = DICKY LAND [sic]

[*On 14 September, Richard had written (in pencil) his first proper letter to Bobbie in 3½ years, which he posted after arrival in Madras on 20th September.*]

14.9.45

My dearest Bobbie,

It is a strange business starting to write letters again after 3½ years and it is a bit difficult trying to sort out one's ideas, especially as one does not know where we are being taken to. Anyway at the moment I am on board a hospital ship 'somewhere in the Indian Ocean' – on the way, we think, to Madras, but there seems to be a remote chance that we may end up in Colombo. I can only hope that the remote chance comes off, as, if I am once 'hospitalised' in India – probably Bangalore – God knows what chance I will have of seeing you. At the moment I am merely convalescent and with reasonable luck I shall be out of the hands of the medical authorities quite soon, which may give me a little more freedom of movement. I feel now that I am caught up in the coils of a friendly, but none the less inexorable machine, which cannot possibly cater for the needs and fancies of the individual in the matter of the route by which he goes home. My present feeling is to get home as soon as possible, if only to find out how I react to people and things at home after being away for so long, but if it can possibly be worked I do want to see you on the way so very badly. Maybe by the time I get the chance of posting this I shall be able to let you know something a little more definite.

From all this you will have gathered that I got your message from RAPWI before I left Singapore. [*Recovery of Allied Prisoners of War and Internees – an Allied military organisation responsible for tracking down the PoW and Internment Camps and providing assistance and support to former PoWs and internees.*] It must have been one of the very first messages to come in, for I got it within the first two or three days of the first paratroops arriving, so you can imagine how very pleased and proud I was to get it.

I expect that by now you will have had access to nominal rolls and casualty lists and will know that poor Sherwood died in Burma in 1943 – one of the many victims of the Thai-Burma Railway. A lot of capital has been made out of that business for propaganda purposes and I am afraid that in the main the stories have not been exaggerated, so you will have an idea of what Sherwood had to go through before he died. I was in the same camp as he was until about 10 days before he died, when he was moved to a so-called Hospital Camp on the Burma side. It was a terribly rough journey even by Japanese standards (I did the same journey a little later myself) and I am afraid it was the journey that killed him. I suppose that Betty will be notified officially in the ordinary way but I will get a letter off to her at the first opportunity – poor Betty, a pretty gloomy Victory for her. [*Richard wrote to Betty Connor on 18 September, a letter her son George only saw for the first time in November 2018. Private George Sherwood Connor, of the Singapore Straits Volunteer Force, is buried at the Thanbyuzayat Commonwealth War Graves Commission cemetery, forty miles south of Moulmein in Burma.*]

For myself I had a pretty good run, except for a pretty rough 8 months on the Thai-Burma Railway. We left Singapore in April 1943 and by the end of the year we were just about useless as a labour force, even by Nip standards, and most of us were back in Changi by Christmas 1943. Up till a couple of months ago I kept as fit as anyone, but then got a bad go of malaria, followed by a most rebellious tummy and so here I am making my way peacefully across the Bay of Bengal in a hospital ship – tummy no longer rebellious now that it is being given some reasonable food.

Your letters came in spasmodically and very late; altogether I got 27 letters or postcards from you (average time in transit 12 months) but they were nonetheless very welcome for that. It was so very brave of you to keep on writing cheerfully and hopefully month after month when you were getting nothing in reply. In that respect you people had the rough end of the stick for you had nothing but uncertainty and, as time went on, I suppose, a growing realisation of the nature of 'our little yellow friends'. Anyway, dearest Bobbie, thank you more than I can properly express for all those letters and for the pleasure and hope which they gave me.

I am afraid that this letter is all taken up with 'I'; how about you? How about your mother? I do hope that by now you will have news of her. I can only offer you my very sincere sympathy about your father, and anyway sympathy to me always seems so inadequate unless I can put it into some practical form.

I feel it is no use writing anymore for the time being, until I know a bit more definitely what is going to happen to me when we get to wherever we are bound for, but I hope to be able to add a bit to this letter before I post it to clear the air a bit.

18.9.45

We are due to disembark tomorrow at Madras for Bangalore; the only address we have been given up to date is:

c/o Recovered PW Mail Centre, Bombay

I imagine however that it is quite possible that you in your exalted position will have very much more up to date information!

Your address is a bit of a problem as I only have the one which came with the RAPWI message; as far as I can find out it is not now considered a desperate secret, so I can only hope that this gets to you safely and that I am not letting you in for trouble for letting out vital military secrets.

No more for now, dearest Bobbie. Goodbye for the present and God bless you.

Dickie

When we did arrive in Madras we got a tremendous welcome from all the ships in the harbour, dressed overall and sounding their sirens like mad. That evening we were put on a Hospital Train for Bangalore, but before we left I had a wonderful piece of good luck. I was recognised and greeted by Joan Vickers (later Dame Joan Vickers), the very good-looking sister of Ralph Vickers of Cambridge/Brooklands/Donnington days (Joan having some quite important job with Red Cross/St. John's Ambulance). [*Joan Vickers was the Chief Welfare Officer, South East Asia Command, with the British Red Cross and the Order of St John. Shortly after Richard saw her, she moved to Batavia to help British troops and prisoners, and also worked in Dutch, Indonesian and Chinese hospitals. She was awarded the Netherlands Red Cross Order of Merit and appointed MBE in 1946. In 1955 she became the MP for Plymouth Devonport, defeating the Labour candidate, Michael Foot, by 100 votes. She held the seat until 1974 when she was succeeded by Dr David Owen. She was created a life peer, Baroness Vickers, in 1975.*] She made special arrangements for me to send a telegram to Bobbie in Colombo, and to expedite a letter to her which I had written on the ship, the first communication from my side which I had been able to send out since we parted on 30th January 1942. I also asked Joan if I could have a bottle of beer (which had been forbidden on the ship), but to my disgust I could not drink more than a small half glass. So much for my dreams, when especially hungry, of three good meals a day (breakfast, lunch and dinner) each consisting of porridge, grilled kipper, bacon and eggs, toast and marmalade and all washed down with breakfast coffee!

Bangalore was a brand new (in fact only partially completed) hospital which had been specially built for the casualties expected from the invasion of Malaya which, but for the Hiroshima/Nagasaki Atomic Bombs, was due to go in shortly. The Hospital at Bangalore was still 'shaking down' but we were extremely well looked after, and after being given a very thorough going over and courses of Mepacrin, Atebrin etc (and a good diet) were soon well on the way to recovery (apart from turning a vivid hue of yellow, brought on by the anti-malarial drugs). In my case the 'thorough going over' was carried out by a lady doctor in the RAMC who was both professionally very competent and very sympathetic.

The next problem was to get permission to go home via Colombo in order to see Bobbie. At first I got a flat 'NO' from RAPWI (sometimes cynically, and rather unfairly, known by a lot of impatient POWs as 'Retain All Prisoners of War Indefinitely'). My opening gambit of wanting to go home via Colombo to see a very dear friend who had written to me every month for the past 3½ years (we were only unofficially engaged) did not achieve the desired result, so I promoted Bobbie to the official status of 'Fiancée' and told her what I had let her in for! This did the trick and I was given permission to go down to Colombo by the first available flight after the Hospital declared me fit.

Whilst all this was going on Bobbie and I were exchanging letters every 3 or 4 days which, on the whole, got through quite quickly. The frequency of this correspondence was soon spotted by the Ward Sister and others who, in the immediate post-war euphoria, found it only too easy to turn our so-called unofficial engagement into a full-scale romance.

[*During the 4 weeks he was in Hospital in Bangalore, Dickie and Bobbie wrote many letters to each other, revelling in his survival and their being in touch again, trying to work out how to meet up, and how to find out about their many friends and relations who had been caught up in the chaos of the war. In the comparatively sheltered and orderly times in which we now live, it is very difficult to imagine how life must have been like then. These are extracts from some of those letters.*]

[*Letter from Bobbie to Dickie, in response to his letter written on the Hospital Ship and posted on arrival in Madras on 20 September.*]

Colombo, Sept 24

My darling Dickie,

Forgive me for typing this – your letter has just arrived. I wrote to you a couple of days ago saying that someone was going to Bangalore and would try to deliver this for me. I've got to give him the letter this afternoon – in a very short time – and thought I would like to try and answer your letter briefly. I'll do it properly when I've got a more definite address, but I am so hoping you will be able to come here. I have only been here six weeks myself so it is rather wonderful that we have been able to make contact so soon. Please try very hard to come here – the Powers That Be are in some ways quite kindly towards ex-POWs, and if you do I would certainly apply for a few days leave, which I am sure I would get in the circumstances. I'm terribly pleased you got my message in Singapore. Until I got your cable the other day I have never known where you were, and just sent mail in the off-chance you might get it; I'm delighted to hear so much got through.

The address you put on the cable and letter is quite OK and will always get me. I can't bear to think of all you have gone through and am so very, very thankful that it is over and you have come through safely. Le Bon Dieu must have listened to me sometimes!

I have seen no nominal rolls or anything so you are the first to tell me about Sherwood. I feel so unhappy about it. I am glad you were with him, please write to Betty as soon as you can (her address is 'Brucefield', Olinda, Victoria, Australia) or care of Sherwood's office. She planned to remain in Australia until she heard of Sherwood. I wrote to her the other day telling her that I was trying to find out about you and Sherwood and that I had found out about you but nothing of Sherwood, which made me think perhaps he might have gone to Australia. Their little boy George is a very bonny kid – I think I probably told you he is my godson – and when you asked him where his Daddy was he used to say very firmly 'in Singapore'. As far as I know Betty only had one card from Sherwood. Tony, her brother who was a POW in Germany, is back and very well. He arrived just after I left so I didn't see him – Betty's last letter said he is to be married very shortly.

I had lunch today with two ex-internees from S'pore and was amazed at how well they looked, and so full of beans too.

Dickie dear this is an awfully feeble letter, but it will have to do just for the moment.

God Bless you darling Dickie, Bobbie

[*Letter from Dickie to Bobbie, in response to hers of 24 September.*]

107 British General Hospital,
Bangalore
28.9.45

Bobbie darling,

Yesterday morning some bright and chatty near-matron of the British Red Cross comes prancing into the Ward and says 'Captain Laird, a love letter for you'. Says Captain Laird, before seeing the letter, 'You may be right', and sure enough she was, so now all the Ward knows that Laird has a 'sweetie' in Colombo. It's not that I'm ashamed of having a 'sweetie' in Colombo; I reckon I'm mighty lucky, but you do feel such a clot when people start shouting abroad your affairs.

Your letter was quite the best thing that has happened since I saw you last. I am afraid I react to news a bit more cautiously than most, and even when the first news of the Nip surrender came through, I couldn't help treating it with reserve, because it seemed so very far from being cut and dried. But something like your letter is real and definite, so that my earth-bound mind can grasp it. God bless you, darling Bobbie, for making me so happy; even physically I feel a mile better already. All this seems so inadequate but some day I'll be able to explain it to you properly.

We are entitled to 42 days repatriation leave, all or part of which can be spent in India; whether India includes Ceylon within the meaning of the act I don't know, but I shall be very surprised if it doesn't in the case of Captain Laird. What I am hoping to arrange is about 3 weeks leave in Ceylon and try and get a ship direct home from Colombo. I've nothing against air travel, but I think that ship is so much more comfortable and pleasant – a sign of advancing middle age or 'last-generationism' I suppose!

And now having said nothing I've reached the end of the airmail paper, so goodbye and God bless you dearest heart.   Dickie

[*Before receiving this letter, Bobbie wrote again to Dickie.*]

29/9/45

Darlingest Dickie,

Seriously, I am sure if you tell them (I don't quite know who I mean by the mysterious 'them') you must visit Colombo before you leave for home they will fix it. I do want to see you so very much. Dash it all your photograph has been grinning at me daily for the last 3½ years, it's high time I saw the original!

I have not had any direct news of Shanghai yet, but a letter from one of Dad's sisters said she had received an air mail from Mum dated 3/9/45, in which she ends up by saying she hoped to get some affairs settled and then leave for good, so it does not sound as if she is going to grab the first ship out. Today I received a letter from a man in Australia who made a hobby of picking up messages from Jap-controlled radios and letting people have them. He picked one up from S'hai for me reading 'Well and safe hope release soon love to all – Mother'. I met a very nice Red Cross man in the Hotel who is en route to China, and he has promised to find out about Mum and do what he can to help her. He has sent a cable for me to the Red X man in S'hai about Mum.

I have written to Betty today and told her that as you got lots of letters from me Sherwood is sure to have received a good few from her. I don't suppose he did if he died in 1943, but it might help her a tiny scrap and I don't know of anything else at the moment. Dickie dear I can't tell you how thrilled I am that you are safe and being well looked after; sometimes wonder if this is all a dream and I'll wake up and find it not there.

Until next time darling, my love to you, Bobbie

[*Letter from Bobbie to Dickie, on receiving his letter of 28 September*]

2/10/45

Dickie my darling,

I'm wildly excited! Your letter of 28th has just arrived – we've established contact at last! I've got such a shaky hand I can hardly write. Silly isn't it. Sorry about the 'love letter' being noised abroad! It just couldn't be helped and was quite unintentional. My sentiments about having one's affairs noised abroad are as yours.

Dickie, how marvellous about your leave. As soon as I know exactly when you will be fit enough to have it I'll apply for some – if I can't get it any other way I'll ask for 'compassionate leave'! I believe one can get a week after 3 months. Anyhow when you are stronger we can get that part of it organised – I've only done about 2 months here but I didn't have any embarkation leave before sailing from Australia.

By the way darling sea travel nowadays is quite different from what it was pre-war so don't get very disappointed if it does not come up to expectations! Personally I'm all for boats at present as once you get parted from your luggage it takes an awfully long time to catch up with you!

You come to the end of these air mail things too quickly.

Keep smiling dearest Dickie, Bobbie

[*Letter from Bobbie to Dickie, two days later*]

4/10/45

Dickie my dearest,

Just received your letter of 1st. I've quite made up my mind you are coming here and if you can't work it I'll be frightfully disappointed. I'm sure if the powers that be knew all the circumstances they would somehow arrange for you to get a ship from here.

Should we not meet here when on earth will we ever see each other? And not to see you now is just unthinkable. When my outfit winds up I'll get repatriated, so it's quite simple for me to get to whatever country I ask to be repatriated to, but once having got there it would be very difficult to move again from what I gather about shipping, because then I would be a single civilian with no priority!

Darling I'm sure you wrote Betty a lovely letter – I wrote to her too and somehow didn't find it a difficult thing to do at all. Usually such letters are awfully hard to write.

Darling, are you feeling better? I ramble on and never ask after your health. I hope the Boys are progressing well too.

Until next time my love, Yours, Bobbie

[*The next day*]

5/10/45

Darlingest Dickie

Tell me the names of the people you are anxious to find out about, and I'll write to R.A.P.W.I. for you if you haven't already done so and I'll also ask anyone I come across; one sometimes does hear that way. I had a note from R.A.P.W.I. the other day to say you had been recovered at Singapore, but they couldn't tell me anymore! I thanked them and told them where you are! They have not been able to find out anything about Mother, so I told them she was known to be in Shanghai early in September, but I would be glad if they could find out anything more for me. Her sister in Sydney is awfully keen for her to go and stay with them which I think is an excellent idea because MUM's sister has a delightful home and garden – I spent one of my brief leaves there.

There are masses of questions I want to ask you but they will have to wait until we meet. Fate could not be so rotten as to bring me here and not let me see you. God Bless darling. Tell the Boys to keep smiling.   Yours always, Bobbie

[*Letter from Bobbie to Dickie, a few days later*]

8/10/45

Dickie my dearest,

It's wonderful to hear that you are beginning to feel really well again and putting on weight. Don't get too ambitious and try pushing over mountains yet.

Capt Laird's fiancée will be terrifically thrilled to see him and will certainly tell any powers that be if the subject is brought up. Letters seem to be taking an average of four days to come through so when you do get permission you'd better send me a wire so that I can apply for a spot of leave and would you also indicate if you want me to fix accommodation for you. If that is the case I'll wire you and let you know where to go, but if by any chance you miss my wire will you enquire for me at the Galle Face Hotel, which you probably know from the days before the war.

I was trying to remember the other day whether you wore glasses or not. I still smile to the wrong people and look straight through the ones I do know!

Darling I can't sit down and write a sensible letter; much too excited at the prospect of seeing you.

Byee for now, my love always, Bobbie

[*Letter from Bobbie to Dickie*]

11/10/45

Dickie my darlingest,

You know I really shouldn't answer your letters the moment I get them because my hand gets so shaky I can barely cope with a pen – this time I have foxed you and am using the old machine to start off with at any rate, although I may finish this in mine own fair hand!

About five minutes after I got two letters from you (one of 4th and the other of 6th) our OC Civilian Women floated by, so I thought 'this is it' – promptly asked for a week's leave (plus an odd day or so) as my fiancé was coming down here on leave and told her briefly (very briefly) the circumstances, also that I could not give a specific date at the moment. She said that was OK and it could be arranged. Things are beginning to take shape now that we have both got verbal Oks for our leaves.

Some of the POWs here had a bit of a job to get enough funds I believe. I have no idea whether you have had any complications in that direction but if you have I could help tide you over. I thought it would be a good idea just to let you know. I seem to recollect once telling you that I would trust you to the end of the world; that still holds good.

I had a letter from Betty today dated 2/10 and she obviously had not heard from either you or me. She has had nothing official and I gather Douglas Johnson told her what had happened but had no details as he was not in Thailand himself I don't think. Betty said she didn't know how to get on to anyone who was with Sherwood. Her letter was quite short – I'm afraid she's very broken up. All the letters Sherwood's two sisters sent him in 1942 & 43 were returned to them marked 'deceased' – their first intimation of anything definite. Betty ended her letter by saying she was going to New Zealand right away. I am sure Betty will have got our letters (I have sent about 3) before she left for NZ and I know she will be relieved to know you were with Sherwood. Good-night darling, My love, Bobbie

[*Betty Connor did go to New Zealand, where Sherwood's family were. Her son George, Bobbie's godson, was raised there. In time he entered the Anglican church, was ordained in 1966, and retired as the Bishop of Dunedin in 2009.*]

[*Later, Bobbie was to be told that her first cousin, Lance Sergeant Jack Garvin (son of her uncle Ernest Garvin), of the 2/19 Battalion AIF, had died in Borneo as a PoW on 4 June 1945 during the notorious Sandakan*

Death Marches. Following the surrender of Singapore in February 1942, over 2,000 Australian and British PoWs were transferred to Sandakan in Borneo to construct an airfield. Conditions there were particularly harsh, and following the completion of the airfield the Japanese force-marched all the surviving prisoners 260 kilometres to Ranau. Of the 2,345 prisoners originally at Sandakan, only 6 survived, all of whom were escapees. Of these, only 4 survived long enough after the war to give evidence at war crimes trials in early 1946, at which 3 Japanese officers were found guilty and subsequently hanged or shot. Jack Garvin is buried in the Labuan War Cemetery, Borneo.]

[*Letter from Bobbie to Dickie, the following day*]

12/10/45

Dickie dearest,

What fun, another letter from you (dated 9th). To write to you is in some small measure to be with you, and to be with you is the nicest thing.

The achievements of the people of Britain fill me with admiration and make me rather proud of being British, but because I didn't actually share in their hardships I'm quite glad that I was not in England for VE day; I would have felt rather a fraud. Does that sound very confused to you? I am glad that you are no longer bitter about Malaya; someday I suppose we will be told why it was so. [*A reference to the ease with which the Japanese evicted the British forces from Malaya.*] I was reading an awfully interesting account in the London 'Times' of the tremendous welcome the British were given on their return there. I had also heard similar stories from ex-internees, so it can't all be propaganda.

Darling Dickie I'm afraid my letters are awfully scrappy and possibly a bit incoherent at times, but the prospect of seeing you soon after this long time leaves me sort of floating on air and I cannot put pen to paper to write a 'good' letter. It's good to know that you are feeling so fit. I saw in the 'Times' that you were 'safe in British hands'. Love to the Boys and for you, well I'll leave that to your imagination!

Yours, Bobbie

After about 4 weeks of rest and good food (and some toning up exercises) I was pronounced fit to leave hospital and within a week, I think on 24th October, I was on a plane down to Colombo. It was a hard-used RAF DC3 (Dakota) stripped down to essentials for supply dropping; no seats apart from vestigial benches along the side of the fuselage and no doors. Not that I had any qualms about the robustness and reliability of this aircraft; and we duly arrived safely in Ceylon.

Bobbie was billeted in the Galle Face Hotel in Colombo and had arranged accommodation for me there, and our 'unofficial' engagement, which for RAPWI purposes was already 'official', was quickly made 'official' for our own purposes! Bobbie had rather wondered whether she would be greeted by a 'Belsen-type' case and was quite surprised to find me looking not much different from when we said 'Good-bye' to each other on Collyer Quay, Singapore, more than 3½ years ago. Bobbie greeted me rather apologetically saying 'I am afraid I have gone rather grey', but I found it very becoming. I have often wondered whether the grey hair was due to the fact that in some ways she had had a worse time than I had, in that I was regularly getting her letters (27 in all during those 3½ years, which must have been almost a record) whereas I was not able to get anything through to her. All she knew (via an enquiry to the 'Sun' Head Office in London) was that at the time of the fall of Singapore I was a POW. All those 25 word letters sent off into the blue month after month represented a very great act of faith. For my part I knew from her letters that she had got through to Australia; for some reason which I have never worked out (telepathy?) I never had any doubt that she would do so. On my side, I lived from day to day, but had considerable faith in my ability to survive whatever the Nips might throw at us POWs.

I do indeed believe that 'Le Bon Dieu/der lieber Gott' had Bobbie and myself in his care.

March 1988   Richard Laird

Postscript

Richard and Bobbie spent some time together in Colombo, during which Bobbie was released from service by Force 136. They both managed to obtain berths on a troop ship returning to England, and arrived there in December 1945. They were married in St. Marylebone Registry Office on 5 January 1946. Following an extended period of leave, Richard was finally released from the Army on 1 August 1946.

They both found post-war England in 1946 a rather unfamiliar place, so decided to return to Singapore, of which, despite all that had happened, they both had good memories. Richard was offered a post in the Sun Insurance office in Singapore, and they arrived back there in early July 1946. Singapore was still then in a rather chaotic state, but they eventually managed to rent a nice colonial-style bungalow in Ewe Boon Road, off the Bukit Timah Road, and settled down there. Their son Rory was born in November 1947. Richard's job involved travel throughout Malaya, often by air. With the Emergency (the Communist insurgency) by now gathering pace, travel by car was not altogether safe; he always travelled with a revolver in the glove box of his car. Holidays in Cameron Highlands and Penang were a welcome distraction. They returned to England in 1949 for six months of home leave (as was normal then for Far East employees of UK-based companies). Instead of catching the ship home from Singapore, they spent a week or so in Penang, staying at a delightful beach-side hotel on Batu Ferringhi Beach called the Lone Pine, before picking up the ship there for the three week voyage home to England. In 1949 the Lone Pine was a simple ten-bedroom bungalow (with outside bath tubs); now it is a (still delightful) luxury hotel (still with outside bath tubs on the room verandahs!).

In 1951, they decided to return permanently to England, and arrived back on New Year's Day 1952. Richard was posted to the Sun Insurance office in Reading, and they soon bought a house in a village in the Thames Valley. They still found it difficult to settle in England, and in the mid-1950s applied to emigrate to New Zealand. Richard was offered a job in the Sun Insurance office in Auckland, and all seemed set, however at the last minute the New Zealand government turned down his application on the grounds of his wartime medical record, having had a host of tropical diseases. (He subsequently lived to the age of 96!)

Thereafter they settled permanently in the Thames Valley, to enjoy a quiet life that reflected their gratitude at having survived the war. Richard never owned another motorbike, but his love of hill-walking, fell-foxhunting and gardening stayed with him for the rest of his life. In some respects my father was fortunate in that, unlike many survivors of Changi and the Railway, he was, as he grew older, able to talk about his experiences. He ascribed his survival of the Burma Railway to three factors. Firstly, aged 32 he was slightly older than many of the young soldiers, and was probably in his prime both physically and mentally. Secondly he had been in the Far East for over five years, and had experience of the jungle in northern Malaya; he was well acclimatized in contrast to the men of 18th Division who had only landed in Singapore between 17 and 29 January, barely three weeks before the fall of Singapore. And finally, he was a small man – as he said, he did not need so much rice to keep him going!

He built up an extensive library of books about the war in Malaya and the Dutch East Indies, and the Far East prisoner of war experience. He was regularly in contact with many of the authors, notably Jim Bradley, the Songkurai escapee (*Towards the Setting Sun* and *The Tall Man Who Never Slept*), Don Wall (*The Heroes of 'F' Force*), and Geoffrey Brooke (*Singapore's Dunkirk*). However he never overcame his intense dislike for the Japanese, and to the end of his life he would not have any Japanese-made product in his house.

My mother died in 1994 and my father survived her by thirteen years, dying peacefully in Scotland in 2008. This book is their memorial.

Appendix I

Narrative of 'F' Force in Thailand, April – December 1943

By Captain Cyril H.D. Wild, Ox & Bucks Light Infantry

[*This narrative report was prepared by Cyril Wild after the survivors of 'F' Force returned to Changi. It was subsequently used in support of the "F" Force Burma-Siam Railway War Crimes Trial' held in Singapore in September 1946. Spellings and use of capitals are as in the original narrative. The original is held within the Imperial War Museum's Colonel Cyril Wild collection (Documents 18752), and is reproduced here with the kind permission of his family.*]

In April 1943, Major-General ARIMURA, GOC Allied Prisoners-of-War in Malaya, issued orders that 'F' Force, to be composed of 3,600 Australians and 3,400 British, should proceed by rail from CHANGI CAMP, SINGAPORE, to a northern destination. These orders further stated that 30% of the 7,000 were to be unfit men. In answer to enquiries, Major-General ARIMURA's Headquarters explained that the journey would entail no marching, and that the force was not required for labour, that food would be abundant, and the unfit men would have a better chance of recovery than at CHANGI. These orders, and the shortage of fit personnel at CHANGI, caused the inclusion in the force of 2,000 unfit men, while the remaining 5,000 also had had some kind of medical history since the capitulation, many of them being recent convalescents from such diseases as diphtheria, dysentery and beri-beri. All were reduced in strength already by malnutrition during the previous year, and the promise of better food and treatment put everyone in high spirits at departure.

The Force entrained at SINGAPORE during the latter part of April 1943 in 13 separate parties at one day intervals, and proceeded, crowded into steel rice trucks, 27 men to a truck, to BAMPONG in THAILAND. The train journey lasted 4/5 days. Food and water were scarce throughout and none were available during the last 24 hours of the journey.

As each party arrived at BAMPONG it learnt that the Force was faced with a march of indefinite length as no transport was available. Consequently all the heavy equipment of the Force, including hospital equipment, medical supplies, tools and cooking gear, and all personal kit which could not be carried on the man, had to be abandoned in an unguarded dump at BAMPONG. Practically the whole of this material (including three quarters of the medical stores) was lost to the Force throughout the 8 months spent up-country, as the immediate advent of the monsoon (at the usual season) prevented the Japanese from moving more than a negligible proportion of it by lorry.

The march of 300 kilometres which followed would have been arduous for fit troops in normal times. For this Force, burdened with its sick and short of food, it proved a trial of unparalleled severity. The road had a loose metal surface for the first two stages but then degenerated into an old elephant track, widened into a hazardous dry weather trail, through dense and mountainous jungle. The march was carried out in stages of 20 to 30 kilometres and lasted 2½ weeks. The parties always marched at night; the monsoon broke in earnest soon after the march began, and conditions rapidly worsened. Everyone was loaded to capacity and such medical equipment of the Force as could be carried was distributed to individuals. Men toiled through the pitch blackness and torrential rain, sometimes knee-deep in water, sometimes staggering off bridges in the dark; sprains and bruises were common, fractures of arms and legs occurred, and stragglers were

Narrative of 'F' Force in Thailand, April – December 1943   147

set upon and looted by marauding Thais. Of the large and growing number of sick, many fell by the wayside, and they and their kit had to be carried by their comrades.

At the staging-camps, which were merely roadside clearings in the jungle, there was no overhead cover; it was sometimes a long carry for water, and it was impossible for men to rest properly. Food generally consisted of rice and onion stew with hot water to drink, and often of rice only.

This was insufficient to maintain health and entirely inadequate to support the physical strain of a march of this description. These staging-camps were in the charge of truculent Japanese NCOs, who demanded large fatigue-parties when the men should have been resting and forcibly drove the sick onto the road with blows to continue the march night after night, in spite of the protests of their officers.

On arrival at the destination (five jungle-camps spread over a distance of 50 kilos – in close proximity to the THAILAND-BURMA border), it was found that the camps had not been completed; and all ranks were housed in un-roofed huts, exposed to the continual downpour of the monsoon rains, which continued without intermission for the next five months. From most of these camps men were taken out to work by the Japanese Engineers as soon as they arrived, without opportunity to rest, although many of them had just completed six successive night marches, and were in the last stages of exhaustion.

Unlike all other Ps.O.W. in THAILAND, 'F' Force remained nominally under the administration of Major-General ARIMURA's headquarters in CHANGI, SINGAPORE. The local Japanese Commander was Lt. Col. BANNO, who proved incapable of either administering the Force or of protecting its personnel from the outrageous demands and treatment of the Japanese Engineers, under whom it was put to work. The camps were commanded by junior Japanese Officers or N.C.O.s of the MALAYA P.O.W. Administration and the guards were Koreans. The former, with one exception, were entirely subservient to the engineers, or themselves actively hostile, while some of the Koreans also treated the prisoners with senseless cruelty. The Officers and men of the engineers, whose sole responsibility to the prisoners was to make them work, behaved with calculated and extreme brutality from start to finish.

Cholera broke out in the first camp early in May. This was directly attributable to the criminal negligence of the Japanese. For at KONKOITA, the last staging-camp but two, every one of the fifteen marching-parties was forced to camp, for one or two days, within yards of huts filled with hundreds of cholera-stricken coolies, on ground covered with infected faeces, where the air was black with flies. British officers asked for the loan of spades to remove this filth, but the Japanese replied contemptuously, 'use your hands'. Lt. Col. HARRIS protested vigorously to Lt. Col. BANNO, warning him of the inevitable consequences, and demanding that either all forward-movement should be stopped or that the infection-point should be by-passed. But nothing was done; the march forward continued, and by the end of May cholera was epidemic in all five labour camps.

The work demanded of all men, without consideration of their physical condition, was heavy navvy-labour on the rushed construction of a 50-kilos stretch of the BURMA-THAILAND railway, through hilly and flooded jungle, immediately south of the THREE PAGODAS PASS. This work was arduous in the extreme, men having to carry logs far beyond their strength and pile-drive up to their waists in water. The hours were generally from first light to dark, but frequently men were kept out as late as 2.00 a.m. the following morning. Men working in the quarries without boots had their feet badly cut and these cuts developed into tropical ulcers. Through incessant work in deep mud, trench feet became practically universal and rapidly developed into ulcers also.

There were daily beatings of officers and men at work, sometimes even into unconsciousness. These beatings were not for disciplinary purposes but were intended to urge sick and enfeebled men to physical efforts quite beyond their remaining strength, or to punish officers for intervening on their behalf.

Every morning the same grim spectacle was repeated in the various camps of parading men for work at first light. Emerging from their crowded huts or leaky shelters in the pouring rain, even the fitter men appeared gaunt and starving, clad in rags or merely loincloths, most of them bootless and with cut and swollen feet. In addition some 50 or 60 sick men from 'hospital', leaning on sticks or squatting in the mud, would be paraded to complete the quota, and would become the subject of a desperate argument between their Officers and the Japanese engineers. Sometimes all of these, sometimes only a part, would be taken out to work and would leave the camp hobbling on sticks or half-carried by their comrades.

Many of the fitter men had not seen their camp in daylight for many weeks and had had no opportunity of washing themselves or their clothes.

The Ps.O.W. Headquarters, under Lt. Col. S.W. HARRIS, OBE, RA was handicapped by the obstinacy of the Japanese in refusing access to the various camps, and by Lt. Col. BANNO's failure to make protests or to ameliorate conditions himself as required. Written protests and appeals to Major-General ARIMURA were never answered. Only once was direct access to the Regimental Commander of the Engineers obtained, and that by chance, when a personal appeal by Lt. Col. HARRIS and his staff resulted in the postponement of an order which would have caused the immediate and permanent expulsion of 700 desperately sick and dying men from their hospital into open jungle during the worst of the monsoon rains, to make way for a native labour force. This order had already been endorsed by Lt. Col. BANNO's administration.

The hospital, so-called, in every camp was nothing but a dilapidated hut with leaky roof, no walls or lighting, and with split-bamboo flooring on which the men were crammed, their bodies touching one another. In these grossly over-crowded conditions even such few mosquito nets as the Japanese provided could not be used, with the result that over 90% of the Force were speedily infected with malaria. Sleeping-mats and blankets were never made available except in negligible quantities.

The attitude of the Japanese towards the sick was a mixture of callous indifference and active spite: for by their sickness they were regarded as impeding the Japanese war-effort. Two remarks made, at official interviews, by Lieut. FUKUDA, Commander of one of the camps, will serve to illustrate this attitude:-

> 'International Law and the Geneva Convention do not apply if they conflict with the interests of the Japanese Army.'

and again (to a senior Australian Medical Officer) :-

> 'You have in the past spoken somewhat boastfully of the Geneva Convention and humanity. You must remember that you are our prisoners-of-war, that you are in our power, and that under present circumstances these things do not apply.'

Although cholera killed approximately 750 of the Force, by far the most deadly disease was dysentery, aggravated by malnutrition, and generally complicated by malaria or beri-beri or both. Over a long period no food was available for such patients except rice and beans, and the quantities provided for the sick was deliberately reduced by the Japanese to starvation-point in the expressed belief that this would compel them to go out to work. The inevitable result was that hundreds of men died in a condition of extreme emaciation and complete despair.

By the 20th June, two months after leaving CHANGI, only 700 [*out of 7,000*] men of the Force were out at work and most of these were sick, while the remainder, except for the small administrative and medical parties, were lying in improvised 'hospitals' in each of the labour-camps.

Narrative of 'F' Force in Thailand, April – December 1943   151

By the end of July the position of the Force was desperate. Communication between the camps and either BURMA or THAILAND had ceased owing to impassable roads and broken bridges: 1,800 of the Force had died. In one camp alone the following diseases were prevalent:- <u>Cholera, typhus, spinal meningitis, small-pox, diphtheria, jaundice, pneumonia, pleurisy, malaria, dysentery, scabies, beri-beri and tropical ulcers.</u> With the exception of quinine, there were very few drugs and no dressings available throughout the whole area, and hideous tropical ulcers were dressed with banana-leaves and puttees, or with dressings fashioned from old shorts or shirts. The result was that some 70 amputations of limbs were necessary, entirely due to the lack of dressings and because the men suffering from ulcers had been forced out to work by the Japanese. Deaths on one camp alone (SONGKURAI No.2) were then averaging 12 a day, and of the original 1,600 British troops who marched into that camp in May, 1,200 were dead before December [*This was the camp in which Richard spent his time on the Railway*].

By the end of December, when the Force arrived back in SINGAPORE, more than 3,000 men were dead out of the original 7,000 who had set out in April, and 1,000 had been left behind in BURMA or THAILAND, either as sick who were incapable of surviving the journey, or as medical and administrative personnel in charge of them. Of the 3,000 survivors who returned to SINGAPORE, 95% were heavily infected with malaria, 80% were suffering from general debility, and 50% required hospital treatment for a long period, chiefly through dysentery, beri-beri, chronic malaria, skin-disease and malnutrition. Six weeks after their return two Japanese Medical Officers examined these 3,000 survivors, with a view to selecting men for further work on aerodrome-construction. They could find only 125, fit for light duty only.

The events narrated here took place, not in the comparative security of a permanent POW camp but in the remoteness of the

THAILAND jungle, and at the hands of a callous and vindictive enemy; they persisted over a long period, to which at the time no end could be foreseen except the likelihood of death by starvation, ill-treatment and disease. Here was no heat and excitement of war, and yet the hardships and privations endured by all were as bad as any likely to be met with on active service and the casualties were unfortunately at least as great.

In these conditions, the unbroken spirit of the Force, and the steady devotion to duty of many Officers, NCOs and men, themselves often seriously ill, were indeed remarkable.

Captain Cyril H.D. Wild.

(Ox & Bucks L.I.)

Appendix II

Report on Prisoners of War in Thailand May To December 1943

By Lieutenant Colonel F.J. Dillon, OBE, MC,
(AA & QMG 18 DIV.)

[*This report was written by Lt Col Dillon on return to Changi from 'F' Force in late 1943. Lt Col Dillon had been ordered to escape from Singapore on the last-minute and ill-fated evacuation of 13 February 1942. He reached Sumatra, and remained there to assist Lt Col Warren with establishing and operating the escape route to Padang. He, with nine other officers, eventually escaped from Padang in a junk on 16 March, but had the misfortune to be intercepted by the Japanese close to Ceylon on 4 April. He was returned to Singapore, and subsequently joined 'F' Force as the Officer Commanding British troops under Lieutenant Colonel Harris, the overall commander of 'F' Force. He worked closely with Cyril Wild.*

His report on 'F' Force covers much the same ground as Cyril Wild's narrative at Appendix I, however it is written with a very different objective. This report is a formal submission to the Japanese military authorities to try to negotiate an improvement in the conditions and treatment of Allied PoWs in Thailand. While there is some duplication with Cyril Wild's narrative, the style is very different, and it is included to illustrate how British senior officers sought, formally, to do business with the Japanese. Sadly history shows that it had limited practical effect; conditions in the Japanese prisoner of war camps in Thailand, Singapore, Sumatra, Borneo and Japan remained harsh, and generally worsened as the impending Japanese defeat led to increasing food shortages. Spellings and use of capitals are as in the original report. As reproduced here, this report is crown copyright and is now out of copyright.]

Introduction

The representatives of the IJA Military Police have requested a frank report to be made on the recent conditions of POWs in Thailand, with suggestions for the improvement of conditions for POWs generally.

Accordingly this report is made in two parts:-

1. FACTS
2. SUGGESTIONS

Part (1) is neither a complaint nor a protest, but a statement of facts, all of which can be substantiated by officers who were present.

The suggestions in Part (2) are made in the sincere hope that the conditions of POWs will improve in the future, since it is our firm belief that our present experiences have not been in accordance with the policy or intentions of the Imperial Japanese Government in Tokyo or of the Japanese Red Cross, who cannot have been aware of the actual state of affairs in Thailand.

Facts

1. Early in 1943, orders were issued to prepare 7,000 'F' Force POWs for a move by train.
   The order stated that:-

   A. The reason for the move was that the food situation in Singapore was difficult, and that it would be far better in the new place.
   B. This was not a working party.
   C. As there were not 7,000 fit combatants in Changi, 30% of the party were to be 'unfit' men, unfit to march or work. The unfit men would have a better chance of recovery with better food, and in a pleasant hilly country, with good facilities for recreation.

Report on Prisoners of War in Thailand May To December 1943   155

    D. There would be no marching, except for short distances from train to nearby camp, and transport would be provided for baggage, and men unfit to march.
    E. The Band were to be taken.
    F. All tools and cooking gear, and an engine and gear for electric light were to be taken.
    G. Gramaphones, blankets, clothing and mosquito nets would be issued at the new camps.
    H. A good canteen would be available in each camp after three weeks. Canteen supplies for the first three weeks were to be bought with prisoners' money before leaving Singapore.
    I. The party would include a Medical party of about 350 with equipment for a central Hospital of 400 patients, and a medical supply for three months.

2. As each train load arrived at Bampong, (600) in each train, they were informed, to their astonishment, that a march of several days was to be carried out by all men, including the 30% unfit. All kit that men and officers could not carry was to be dumped at Bampong. This amounted to the equivalent of about fifteen railway truck loads of stores and baggage.

3. The march in fact was one of 300 kilometres in 15 stages, and lasted for 2½ weeks. Marching was at night, along rough jungle racks (except for the first two stages) and as all torches had been taken from POWs during the search at Bampong, control by POW officers was difficult and near impossible.

4. After the first stage the unfit men became increasingly ill, and were a handicap to the other men who were at first fairly fit, but rapidly themselves became ill and exhausted as they had to help, and even carry, the increasing number of men who were unable to walk unaided.

5. Conditions at the staging camps were:-

    A. At no stage was overhead cover provided except for a few tents (for 100 men) at the camp. The weather was variable and the rainy season started while the march was in progress.
    B. Food supplies were generally poor, and in many camps had consisted of rice only.
    C. Water was short at many camps, and at Kanburi [*Kanchanaburi*], drinking water had to be bought by the prisoners from a privately

owned well. Colonel Harris (O/C 'F' Force) protested, but the matter was not put right.

    D. No proper arrangements existed for the retaining of sick at these camps, and men who were absolutely unfit to march (owing to disease and sickness) were beaten and driven from camp to camp. Officers, including Medical Officers, who begged and prayed for sick men to be left behind, were themselves beaten at many camps. In one particular case, a Japanese Medical Officer (Lieut.) ordered the IJA Corporal in charge of Tarso camp to leave 36 men behind as they were too ill to move. The Corporal refused to obey this order, although it was repeated in writing, and a British Officer (Major WILD) Interpreter and an Australian Doctor (Major BRUCE HUNT of Perth) were severely beaten when they protested. (I was with this party – a bone in the Doctor's hand was broken.)

        Of these sick men who were compelled to march, nearly all have since died, including an Australian Chaplain who died at the next camp. (The Japanese Medical Officer had particularly stated that the Chaplain should not march, as he was an elderly man with a weak heart and was already at the end of his strength.)

    E. The men marched all night as a rule, from 7 pm to 7 am. They had to perform camp duties, get their meals and wash during the day when water was available, and so had little rest.

6. <u>MEDICAL</u>

    A. Such medical stores as had been hastily selected at Bampong, and carried by hand with the marching parties, were rapidly exhausted and the march continued with no medicines at all.

    B. Dysentery and Diarrhoea broke out in all parties, and exhaustion was general. Ulcerated feet occurred in large numbers, due to sick men with blistered feet being forced to march.

7. At <u>Koncoita</u> the marching parties were quartered in the same camp as a Thai Labour Corps, who were suffering from Cholera. The infection was picked up by each of the 13 parties of the marching prisoners.

8. On 15th May, Cholera broke out at Shimo-Nieke. Colonel Harris, the commander of the POWs immediately reported to Colonel Banno, the IJA Commander, and requested that movement should cease until

the outbreak was under control, and the Koncoita camp should at all costs not be used for further parties. Unfortunately Colonel Banno was unable to comply with this request and, as a result, Cholera was spread into all five work camps occupied by the force.

9. Only a small quantity of Medical supplies at Bampong was brought up later by lorry (over three quarters of it was still at Bampong when the force returned to Canburi [*Kanchanaburi*] in December). The IJA were unable at this time to provide or produce any Medical supplies whatsoever, except Cholera vaccine and Quinine, which was always supplied as required. Colonel Banno gave us six tins of milk of his own property.

10. By the end of May, about 5,000 men had been distributed to several different camps. These consisted of huts, without any roofing, although the rainy season had started fully, and rain was falling heavily during the day and night. The camps were not fully roofed for some weeks during which time the men had no proper shelter. Consequently, deaths from Pneumonia were numerous.

11. In spite of the above conditions, the general state of exhaustion of the men, the presence of the Cholera epidemic in all camps, and practically universal Malaria, Diarrhoea and Dysentery, the men were put to work by the Engineers at once.

12. Maximum numbers of men were taken to work each day. This left insufficient numbers of men in camp for sanitary purposes, and for nursing the sick, while disease increased, disease of every kind. In some camps, Red Cross personnel were forced to go out onto the Road [*railway*], but this was quickly stopped by Colonel Banno.

13. In several camps, a great scarcity of tools made improvements to sanitation difficult or impossible. The tools which the Prisoners had brought from Changi, and which were part of the heavy baggage at Bampong, were never brought up.

14. It was clear to all Officer Prisoners that if the Engineers continued to take all fit men and convalescent men to work each day, there would soon be no men at all fit to work. In fact, the Engineers were rapidly destroying their only available source of labour. This aspect was explained to our own IJA HQ who clearly agreed, but were apparently unable to prevent the Engineers doing as they liked. The task in front of the Engineers and the need for speed were clearly realised by us, but the destruction by the Engineers of their only available labour force was just as bad from their point of view as from ours.

A little common sense on their part could, early in June, have saved the situation for us and themselves. Unfortunately for us this short-sighted policy continued, and by the end of June, only about 700 of the 5,000 men north of Nieke were at work daily, and of these at least half were unfit and useless for heavy work. Of the remainder, except for the Red Cross personnel and a small number of administrative personnel, all men were laying in the hospitals very ill.

15. By this time, the road from the South was impassable, and the road to the North was difficult, and the scale of rations fell to below the level required to keep men fit in health and far below the amount required to help sick men back to health. It has been said that we were on the same rations as the IJA soldiers, but this was not true as can be easily proved. The rations of the men in the hospital were fixed at far too low a scale (250 to 300 Grams of rice, and a small quantity of beans per day). In our opinion this was a great mistake, and we continually said so to the IJA. There seemed to be an idea that the lack of pay and rations would drive the men out of the hospital, but this of course would only happen if the men were not ill. There was however no deception about the illness of our men, for they were dying in large numbers.

16. As the health of the men grew worse, the demands of the Engineers were more and more difficult to meet, and their treatment of our weak and sick men while at work became more and more brutal. The work was often beyond what could be reasonably expected of fit men, and it was certainly beyond the strength of the weak men – this especially relates to the carriage of heavy logs. It was noticed that where there were Thai or Burmese labour used for this task, two or three times the number of our men were used. It became common for our men to be literally driven with wire whips and bamboo sticks throughout the whole working day. Hitting with the fist and kicking also occurred frequently throughout the day. It was emphasised that the beating was not for disciplinary purposes, but was intended to drive unfit men to efforts beyond their strength.

17. The hours of work were also excessive. 14 hours a day was a common occurrence and work went on, day after day, without a break for months. Many men never saw their camps in daylight for weeks on end, and never had a chance to wash themselves or their clothes.

18. In some camps where the number of fit men fell below the Engineers' demands, the Engineers themselves came into the camp, and forced

Report on Prisoners of War in Thailand May To December 1943   159

prisoners out of hospital to work. Except in isolated instances, Officers were not allowed or made to work outside the Camps, but the Engineers often used the threat that Officers would be taken out for work if more men were not turned out of hospital. [*Although, as Richard has described earlier in Chapter 4 of his memoir, at Songkurai No.2 officers were routinely required to work.*]

19. At Songkurai [*Richard's camp*], where conditions were probably worse than anywhere else, the IJA Engineer Officer, Lieut. ABE, himself came into the camp and, asking to see six officers who were most seriously ill (of whom three subsequently died) said 'Unless more men are produced for work tomorrow, I will send my soldiers to take these Officers out to work'. This Engineer Officer was conspicuous at all times in failing to stop brutal treatment of prisoners by his men, even if it happened in his presence. Of the 1,600 men who went to Songkurai camp in May, 1,200 are already dead and 200 more are in hospital, many of whom are not expected to recover. Many petitions and appeals were made to Lieut. Abe but he treated them with contempt. The result would have been even worse if it had not been for the arrival of Lt. Wakabayashi (of the Malaya prisoners of War Administration) in Songkurai camp at the beginning of August [*see also Richard's comments on Lt. Wakabayashi at page 105*] . From this date in that camp, conditions gradually improved.

20. By July, more than half the force were without boots, and this caused a large number of poisoned feet and 'trench foot' from continual work in the wet. Blankets were not issued as promised (at Changi) to men without them. Clothing issues were negligible. Issue of medical stores were totally inadequate. Bandages and dressings were seldom issued, and only in small quantities. For hundreds of Tropical Ulcer cases, dressings were improvised from banana leaves and bandages from sleeves, and legs of pants; consequently, many limbs had to be amputated unnecessarily and many of these patients died.

21. By the end of July, the road to Bampong was still impassable and, although the river was open to traffic and was in use by the IJA and Thai shopkeepers, our medical and other supplies were still not brought up from Bampong, and in the end were never brought up. This was in spite of our repeated protests and requests.

22. It was during the forgoing period that several men, sometimes alone, sometimes in groups, disappeared into the jungle. Some probably

had the idea of escaping, some undoubtedly only left so as to die in freedom, rather than in captivity of disease and illness or ill-treatment. The men on the whole were in despair. The choice in front of them seemed to be death from disease, or never-ending toil and brutal treatment at the hands of the Engineers. The Prisoners' Officers were unable to protect them in spite of all their efforts. One party of Officers, seeing their men dying and ill-treated around them, and in despair at getting any redress from the IJA, attempted to escape so as to let the world know what was happening to the prisoners, and try to get help from the International Red Cross. This party failed as was inevitable. Five perished from privation in the jungle, and the remaining four were re-captured.

23. In August, a hospital was established in Burma, and about 2,000 men sent there. Unfortunately, the rations were still deficient of the necessary vitamins and 800 men died. Nevertheless, the Burma hospital did great good for there was no regular Engineer work, and therefore many men had a chance to get well slowly. [*This was Tanbaya, where Richard was sent.*]

24. From August onwards, things improved at Songkurai but did not improve much at Kami-Songkurai. As late as October for instance, the Engineers were blasting in a quarry just behind the prisoners' hospital in such a way that rocks and stones fell on the hospital huts with each blast. The huts were crammed full with patients, many of whom were dying (about 8 per day were dying). All patients were terrorised, many more or less seriously injured; one man had his arm broken and subsequently died from the combination of the injury and his previous disease. This went on for over a week before representations that were made to the IJA Officer in charge of the camp were successful. Blasting continued in such a way that rocks did not fall on the hospital, thus showing that the previous practice was avoidable. In this camp also, the latrine used by several hundred Tamil labourers was within ten yards of the Prisoner Officer Quarters. The Tamils had suspected Cholera and Smallpox at this time.

25. In all camps, accommodation was totally inadequate. Men actually slept touching each other, and as a result skin disease infection was 100% throughout the force. Most Officers were as badly off as the men.

26. The move back to Kanburi took place in November, but the men were in such a state that (although the worst cases were left in

Burma) 46 died on the train journey, and 146 in the following three weeks, in spite of better food and living conditions. It is certain that several hundred more men will die from the result of their treatment in Thailand during the next month or two.

27. Our own guards, on the whole, treated us well. Face slapping of prisoners of all ranks was discouraged by our IJA Officers, but was still fairly common. It nearly always arose from a language misunderstanding and was not in itself serious, although it makes the maintenance of discipline very difficult for the Prisoner Officers. There are some guards, however, who seem incapable of being put in charge of any task without losing their tempers and hitting prisoners. The most flagrant case is that of a 'Gunshou Toyama', who claims to be a well educated man. At Bampong he hit Officers and men on every party with a heavy steel shafted golf club. He cut one Major's head open, badly damaged another Officer's arm, and severely hurt many others. The cause of these assaults were never known. Later at Shimo-Songkurai and at Kami-Songkurai camps he habitually hit Officers and men for no just cause. He has an ungovernable temper, and is apparently uncontrollable by his own Officers. Apart from actual striking, he was always at pains to be insulting to Officers, especially Senior Officers. Such a man should not be allowed to be in charge of Prisoners.

28. There were many cases latterly in which our own guards prevented Engineers from maltreating prisoners.

29. It may be thought that some of the above report is exaggerated. It is however only the barest outline of a period of intense hardship suffered by a party of Prisoners of War. If proof is wanted, it is surely sufficient to point to the fact that of the 7,000 prisoners who left Changi in April, now in December about 3,000 are dead, and 3,000 more are in hospital or are convalescent patients, of whom hundreds more will die within the next few months from the results of the hardships they have undergone.

30. We know from letters received from England and Australia, that it is believed there that Prisoners of War are being well treated by the Japanese. If the actual facts regarding Thailand were known abroad, the news would be greeted with indignation and amazement.

Suggestions

General

We ask firstly that we should be treated in accordance with the letter and the spirit of the Geneva and Hague Conventions, particularly those of 1906 and 1907, both of which were ratified by Britain and Japan. It has been suggested that the unconditional surrender of Singapore places the prisoners from Singapore outside the terms of the Hague Convention. This is obviously NOT SO. The position of any prisoner who is captured on the field of battle is clearly that of unconditional surrender, but no one would suggest that he is not covered by the Convention. How then, can the nature of the Singapore surrender, (which was correctly made at the written request of General Yamashita 'in order to avoid further useless loss of life on both sides and especially the lives of the civilians of the city') put the garrison of Singapore outside the terms of the Convention?

Detailed Suggestions

The following detailed suggestions are all consequent on the general one:-

1. Doctors and Red Cross personnel are not POWs, and should not be treated as prisoners. (Article 9, Geneva convention, 1907)
2. Prisoners should be humanely treated. (Annex to Hague Convention 1907)
3. Work should not be excessive. (Annex to Hague Convention 1907 – Article 6)
4. Prisoners should be treated as regards rations, quarters and clothing on the same footing as the troops of the Government which captured them. (Annex to Hague Convention 1907 – Article 7)

Notes

1. All the above articles were broken in Thailand.
2. As regards rations, it is not enough just to fix a scale of rations; the essential is that the rations should reach the Prisoners. It is suggested

that the Military Police undertake the duty of seeing that the scale of ration issue allowed does, in fact, reach the Prisoners.
3. As regards Quarters, it should be remembered that Officer Prisoners pay for their Quarters.
4. Officers must not be employed for labour. In Thailand, many hundreds of officers were forced to work on Railway and Road construction. This is without precedent in the history of modern warfare, and will not be forgotten for 100 years.
5. Red Cross representatives should be allowed to visit POW camps. We received no visits in Thailand.
6. Proper arrangements should be made to collect deceased persons gear.
7. Arrangements for letters to and from home should be improved. Our mail arrives a year or more later, and we cannot write a full letter home.

Appendix III

Tanbaya Hospital Burma – Medical Report Aug 1st – Nov 24th 1943

By Major Bruce Hunt, AAMC, Commanding Burma Hospital

[This is an extract from an official report written by Major Bruce Hunt, AAMC, the officer commanding the 'F' Force Hospital established at Tanbaya in Burma. The report was written at Kanchanaburi in late December 1943 after the majority of the patients had been evacuated from Tanbaya.

Owing to the very high levels of sickness in 'F' Force, and the extreme difficulties that the Japanese were having in transporting sufficient food to their northerly work camps at the height of the monsoon, the Japanese took a decision in July 1943 to establish a Hospital Camp seventy kilometres further north in Burma at a former 'A' Force work camp at Tanbaya. This would allow the evacuation of up to 2,000 unfit men to a location that would be easier to supply via the already completed northern section of The Railway. That at least was the theory; Bruce Hunt's report makes it clear that it did not work out quite that way in practice. Spelling and punctuation have been left unchanged from the original. The report is available on many Australian websites; this copy was taken from the website of the 2/26 Battalion AIF.]

Tanbaya Hospital Burma Medical Report
Aug 1st – Nov 24th 1943

Introductory

The IJA [*Imperial Japanese Army*] first intimated (on 29 June) that it was intended to establish a hospital in Burma to receive men from 'F' Force who would be incapable of work for at least two months. Rolls were prepared for a hospital of 2,000, but on 8 July all plans were cancelled. Fresh orders were issued on 21 July to prepare rolls, this time for a 1,250 bed hospital. Lt. Col. Harris, Commanding 'F' Force, had appointed me OC Hospital on 1 July, and on 24 July I was taken to Burma by the IJA in company with Lieut. SAITO, to examine the hospital site. I returned on 28 July, and on 30 July the advance party left for Burma.

General Comment

When the proposal for a Hospital Camp was first mooted hopes ran high that this would be a means of saving hundreds of lives. This was particularly the case amongst hospital patients who by reason of their illnesses might be regarded as eligible for selection for Burma. There seemed reasonable grounds for this enthusiasm as the IJA had given assurances that no work would be demanded from the camp and that the dietary would be a good deal better than it was in the working camps; a further statement had been made that the necessary drugs and medicines would probably be supplied.

The records contained in the War Diary indicate that the hopes at first extended for the success of the camp were not realised. A death rate of 660 (with a possibility of 90 – 100 more) out of a total camp entry of 1,924 is a profoundly disappointing result. The reasons for this high death rate are set out below. It is a melancholy reflection that in November there was as much enthusiasm to leave Burma as there had been in July to go there.

1. State of Diseases

Very many patients were in such an advanced state of disease on arrival in Burma that even with the best hospital facilities in the world recovery would have been impossible. This applied particularly to patients from Songkurai (No.2) camp, where, as we

Tanbaya Hospital Burma – Medical Report Aug 1st – Nov 24th 1943

understand, evacuation of all very sick patients was practically compulsory.

2. State of Nutrition

Apart from the state of their disease, the nutritional state of many of the patients also gravely prejudiced their chance of recovery. In part this was due to poor rations at the working camps, but in part it arose from the failure of medical officers in certain of the working camps to insist on consumption by their sick patients of their full daily ration; in many cases of dysentery liquid diet had been prescribed for an unconscionably long time, resulting in practical starvation of the unfortunate patient. Apart from the emaciation a long-standing deficiency in vitamins A, B1 & 2, and C also greatly lowered the patients' power to combat their disease.

3. Effects of the Journey

The journey was made under very arduous conditions. An inadequate supply of fit men was available to help sick patients – food was poor and long exposure to rain storms and severe jolting were the lot for all. Under these circumstances many patients whose fate hung in the balance had their last chance of survival taken away from them by the strain of the journey. [*Richard made just this point in his Memoir in describing the deaths of Sherwood Connor and the young soldier from the Northumberland Fusiliers.*]

Factors Operative at Tanbaya

1. Diet

So far from the diet being better than at the working camps it was for long periods considerably worse… . Rice was generally adequate, but every other essential for a complete diet was grossly deficient. In particular, until the bean ration was raised from ⅓ of a bag to 1 bag on 22nd September, the diet contained practically no vitamin B or C. Innumerable protests and requests for rice polishings and for more beans were made to the IJA but always met with the answer that rice polishings were unobtainable and that there was a great shortage of beans.... . [*'Polishings' is the brown bran-like dust which is obtained during the polishing process of rice. It consists of the outer skins of the grain, and is high in vitamin B.*] In this connection it was learnt on 10th October that 'A' force Hospital camp, just 5 kilometres away, had been receiving an adequacy of beans since July. When this was pointed out to the IJA Camp Commandant he raised the bean issue to 2½ bags forthwith. It is also interesting to note that from 26th October onwards regular issues of rice polishings were made available to the camp. Had these two steps been taken earlier in the camp's history it is my considered opinion that upwards of 100 lives would have been saved... .

2. Drug Shortages

Until 5th November no drugs were received from the IJA and even then the supply was pitifully small and inadequate. In particular no specific therapy was available for treatment of Amoebic or Bacillary Dysentery, the major killing diseases in the camp. There was no Iodoform or other drug suitable for local treatment of the numerous tropical ulcers. No Sulphur (a common, cheap and easily procurable product) was available to treat scabies until 5th November by which time the whole camp was infected with much secondary suppuration and ulcer formations. Dressings were also woefully deficient and many mosquito nets had to be sacrificed to dress the enormous ulcers. No Iron was available to build up the anaemic patients, and no concentrated B1 was available for the numerous severe Beri Beri cases.

3. Malaria

Tanbaya was an area where Malaria of a particularly severe type was hyperendemic. 87 deaths are shown as being due either wholly or partially to Malaria, but beyond this the disease had a debilitating effect throughout the camp where its incidence reached approximately 100%. In particular Malaria caused marked deterioration in the condition of patients suffering from ulcers or dysentery... .

System of Administration

The system of administration adopted at Tanbaya differed in several respects from that customary in military hospitals. Lt. Col. Hutchinson as Administrative Commandant of the camp was responsible for such services as cooking, securing of wood and water, hygiene and pay; Major Hunt, as OC Hospital, was responsible for all medical treatment and for the administrative control of all medical personnel, professional or amateur, and of all patients.

Patients were segregated so far as was possible according to their complaints; this facilitated their treatment and prevented much cross infection... . Each ward contained in the early stages 190 patients and was under the control of a Wardmaster. The Wardmaster was a combatant officer, usually of Company Commander status or above, and he had as assistants; an assistant Wardmaster, usually a subaltern, 2 NCOs who acted as CSM [*Company Sergeant Major*] and CQMS [*Company Quarter Master Sergeant*] respectively and a clerk. The Wardmaster was responsible for nominal rolls, for discipline, for hut cleanliness, for messing, for canteen supplies and in general for everything which took place in the ward except such matters as involved technical medical knowledge or skill... .

Staff

Although the number of RAMC and AAMC personnel at Tanbaya was at its highest 142, very many of these men arrived as patients and either died at Tanbaya or remained as patients throughout their stay in Burma. The maximum number of Medical Corps personnel available for duty at any one time was 62, but the number generally varied between 40 and 50. Under these circumstances it was necessary for the greater part of the nursing work to be done by volunteers from non-medical units.... Many of the volunteers showed a marked aptitude for the more technical branches of nursing and in some cases were as good as, if not better than, the majority of the professionals.

Disease

Four diseases dominated the clinical picture. These were in order of mortality which they produced, Dysentery, Tropical Ulcers, Beri Beri and Malaria.

1. Dysentery

In the absence of facilities for bacteriological or sigmoidoscopic examination it was impossible in most cases to differentiate between Amoebic and Bacillary Dysentery. Clinically however, I formed the opinion that the former disease predominated.... The Dysentery wards were amongst the most tragic places in the camp. Many of the patients put up a valiant struggle forcing their rice down day after day and week after week in a heroic effort to stay alive until adequate facilities for treatment arrived. Dysentery alone caused 114 deaths, and in association with other diseases played a part in killing 334 men. In many cases an attack or recurrence of Dysentery was the terminal factor in carrying off patients suffering from Beri Beri or Ulcers.

2. Tropical Ulcers

These were of very great frequency and in many cases of horrifying severity. Huge areas of skin, flesh and in some cases bone were eaten away and the skin appeared to possess little or no resistance to the infecting organisms. Ulcers followed small scratches or cuts with distressing frequency and not a few patients died of Ulcers which actually developed in the camp.... The lower extremity, and in particular the region of the Tibia was the most common site of election for the formation of Ulcers. They could, and did however, occur in almost any area of the body.... A few cases

Tanbaya Hospital Burma – Medical Report Aug 1st – Nov 24th 1943   171

responded strikingly to the application of Sulphanilamide or Iodoform [*Richard was one of these fortunate few*], and had these drugs been available in anything like adequate amounts much life would have been saved. In the absence of these drugs simple cleansing with Eusol or Saline two or three times daily provided the best results. Amputations were performed in 60 cases, but here also the results were in general disappointing, owing to the poor general condition of the patients and the frequent occurrence of severe secondary sepsis in the stump.... Ninety two patients died of Ulcers alone and 105 of Ulcers complicated by other diseases.

3. Beri Beri

Beri Beri was widespread throughout the camp, and at one time there were upwards of 600 patients showing clinical manifestations of the disease. It was also more severe than any which I had previously seen.... A further complication which caused much loss of life in Beri Beri was the frequency with which some Beri Beri patients developed a rapidly spreading gangrene in their water logged extremities; this was almost invariably fatal.... Administration of Vitamin B1 intravenously saved a certain number of lives when cardiac emergencies occurred, but of this, as of all other valuable drugs, supplies were grossly inadequate. 68 patients died of Beri Beri alone and in a further 260 cases Beri Beri was one of the causes of death.

4. Malaria

Malaria was practically universal throughout the camp, and in August and September relapses were very frequent, as owing to the shortage of supplies it was not possible to give quinine treatment for longer than 7 days.... After the end of September supplies increased considerably, and it was possible to increase the course... resulting in a marked fall in the incidence of malarial relapses. One of the outstanding clinical features of Malaria at Tanbaya was the high degree of resistance to quinine.

Evacuation

As early as September strong representations were made to the IJA that many hundreds of patients would not successfully survive a long railway journey. As a result of these representations considerable leniency was allowed in the selection of patients to travel. Much care was taken with this selection and as a result, of the 900 patients who left Tanbaya for Kanchanaburi by December 1943 only two failed to survive the arduous 5 to 6 days journey.

After the main evacuation was completed in December 1943, a staff of 102 was left behind in Burma to look after 218 patients. Of these patients, approximately 85 were suffering from Dysentery, 65 from Ulcers and the majority of the remainder had Beri Beri. If the final patients are evacuated in February 1944, as seems probable, I anticipate a mortality of 90/100.

Conclusion

The Burma Hospital Camp for the reasons stated above, could not be regarded as a success. Its partial failure however was much mitigated by the work of the administrative staff, by the devotion to duty of the Wardmasters and by the professional knowledge and skill displayed by some of the medical staff.

KANCHANABURI   (Sgd) Bruce Hunt. Major AAMC
23.12.43   Commanding Burma Hospital

Bibliography and Suggested Further Reading

Bloom, Freddie. *Dear Philip – A Diary of Captivity, Changi 1942/45*, Bodley Head, 1980.

Bowden, Tim. *Changi Photographer – George Aspinall's Record of Captivity*, ABC Enterprises, 1984.

Bradley, James. *Towards the Setting Sun*, J.M.L. Fuller, 1982.

———. *Cyril Wild – The Tall Man Who Never Slept*, Woodfield Publishing, 1991.

Brooke, Geoffrey. *Singapore's Dunkirk*, Pen & Sword, 2003.

Brown, Hamish. *East of West, West of East*, Sandstone Press Ltd, 2018.

Connell, Brian. *The Return of the Tiger*, Doubleday & Co, 1960.

Cordingly, Eric. *Down to Bedrock*, Swallowtail Print, 2013.

Cruickshank, Charles. *SOE in the Far East*, Oxford University Press, 1983.

de Rosario, Lionel. *Nippon Slaves*, Janus Publishing, 1995.

Dewey, Judy and Stuart. *POW Sketchbook*, Pie Powder Press, 1985.

Gough, Richard. *SOE Singapore 1941/1942*, William Kimber, 1985.

Harmsen, Peter. *Shanghai 1937: Stalingrad on the Yangtze*, Casemate, 2013.

Imperial War Museum. *The Burma-Siam Railway – The Secret Diary of Dr Robert Hardie*, IWM, 1983.

Kinvig, Clifford. *Death Railway*, Ballantine Books Inc, 1973.

Lomax, Eric. *Railway Man*, Vintage, 1996.

McKie, Ronald. *The Heroes*, Angus & Robertson, 1960.

Pavillard, Stanley. *Bamboo Doctor*, Macmillan, 1960.

Skidmore, Ian. *Marines Don't Hold Their Horses – Biography of Colonel Alan Warren*, W.H. Allen/Virgin Books, 1981.

Urquhart, Alistair. *The Forgotten Highlander*, Abacus, Little Brown, 2010.

Varley, E. *The Judy Story – The Dog with Six Lives*, Souvenir Press, 1973.

Wall, Don. *Heroes of 'F' Force*, Don Wall Publications, 1993.

Newspapers and Magazines

'Five Months of War', *North-China Daily News & Herald*, 1938.

Wild, Cyril. 'Expedition to Singkep', *Blackwood's Magazine*, 1946.

Index

Abe, Hiroshi, Lieutenant, IJA, 82, 97, 159
AMARAPOORA, SS, Hospital Ship, 126–7
Arimura, Major General, IJA, 145–9
Aspinall, Private George, Australian photographer, xv, 173
ASAMA MARU, Japanese liner, 76, 86
Aucott, Ian, companion on Korean holiday 1938, 24, 27–8
AUGUSTA, USS, American cruiser, 15
Australian Imperial Force (AIF), 54
Ayer Hitan, town in northern Johore, Malaya, 55

Ballment, 'Cocky', Sun Insurance manager, 37
Ban Pong, Thailand, 81, 86–9, 146, 155–9
Bangalore, 107 British General Hospital, 127–8, 130–3
Banno, Lieutenant Colonel, IJA, 83, 147–9, 156–7
Batavia, Java, xiii, 56, 65
Battle of the River Plate, 44

Bell, Captain Frederick Secker ('Hookie'), Royal Navy, 44
Bradley, James ('Jim'):
 books written, 83–4, 142, 173
 escape from Songkurai No.2 Camp, 83, 100, 160
Brankali Camp, Burma Railway, 92
Broome, Colonel Richard, OBE, MC, 52
Brown, Hamish, mountaineer and author, xv, 173

Cameron Highlands, Malaya, 141
Cammell Laird, shipbuilders, xi
Campbell, Major Jock, OBE, 51–2
Cathay Hotel, No.20 The Bund, 2
Changavaya Camp, Burma Railway, 103
Changi:
 Allied air activity 1944–45, 121
 camp activities and services, 116–18
 food and diet, 70, 72–4, 113, 115–16
 life in Changi, 113–14
 news service, 118, 121–2
 Selarang Incident 1942, 74–6
 sport, 77, 113

vegetable gardening, 115–16
  see also Laird, Richard
Chiang Kai-Shek, 121
China United Apartments, 2, 5
Colombo, Ceylon, xiii, 126
Connor, Betty (née Gordon, married to Sherwood), xv, 39, 52, 79–80, 129, 133–8
Connor, George (son of Sherwood and Betty Connor), xv, 80, 138
Connor, Pop (Betty's father), 80
Connor, Sherwood, xv, 39, 79–80, 102, 120, 128–9, 133–5, 138, 167
Cooper, Major, Royal Engineers, 111
Corless, Eric (Joe), Chartered Accountant, 38
CORNWALL, HMS, British cruiser, sinking, 71
Cotterell, Tom, Chartered Accountant, 38
Couper Patrick, Bobbie:
  escape from Singapore to Australia, 63–8
  evacuation to Hong Kong, 12
  family, xiii
  godmother to George Connor, 80
  letters to Dickie following release, 132–9
  move to Singapore, 1941, xiii, 52
  work with Special Operations Executive (SOE), xiii, 68
Couper Patrick, Dr Harry:
  death in Shanghai 1942, 120
  father of Bobbie Couper Patrick, xiii
  Medical Officer to Shanghai Scottish, 12
  Medical Superintendent Shanghai General Hospital, 16, 120
  Surgeon to the Lester Chinese Hospital, 120
Cyril Wild – The Tall Man Who Never Slept, by James Bradley, 83, 173

DAINTY, HMS, British destroyer, 12
Dalton, Hugh, Minister of Economic Warfare, 1940, 36
Davis, Lieutenant Colonel John, CBE, DSO, 51–2
Des Indes Hotel, Batavia, 66–7
DEVONSHIRE, HMS, British cruiser, sinking, 71
Diamond Mountains, *Kumgangsan*, (Korea), 24–31
Dillon, F.J., Lieutenant Colonel, OBE, MC, 115, 153
Dobson, Major R.W. ('Dobbie), RASC, 57, 61, 86
DUCHESS OF BEDFORD, SS, 57
Duckworth, Noel, Chaplain 'F' Force, 85

EMPIRE STAR, Blue Funnel Line, 59
EMPRESS OF ASIA, 12, 102
EXETER, HMS, British cruiser, 44, 67–8

Exmouth Gulf, Western
    Australia, 109

Faraday, Barbara ('Barbie'):
    marriage to Henry Laird, 1929, xi
    financial support after Henry's
        death, 47
FELIX ROUSSEL, Messageries
    Marine, 59, 103
First Opium War, 1
Flying Boats:
    'C' Class Empire, 48
    Catalina, 49
    Short Singapore, 48
Fremantle, Australia, 68
Fukuda, Lieutenant, IJA, 150

Galle Face Hotel, Colombo, 123,
    137, 140
Gammeters, Watch Shop, Collyers
    Quay, 56, 123
Garvin, Ida, mother of Bobbie
    Couper Patrick, xiii
Garvin, Lance Sergeant Jack,
    2/19 Battalion AIF, 138
Gatey, Colin, Naval Officer:
    father, Norman Gatey (Gatey
        Heelis solicitors), xi
    marriage to Maudie Laird,
        1929, xi
    Senior Engineer, HMS
        QUEEN ELIZABETH,
        1937, 8
Geneva Convention, 150, 162
Genuang Station, northern
    Johore, Malaya, 54

Goode, Sir William ('Bill'), 76–7
GNEISENAU, German
    battlecruiser, 33
GRAF SPEE, German pocket
    battleship, 44
Green, Peggy and Bobbie, 58
Grik, Malayan town in Perak
    state, 47

Haadyi, Malaya, 89
Hague Convention, 162
Hangchow, 15
Harris, Lieutenant Colonel S.W.,
    OBE, Royal Artillery, 100,
    148–9, 153, 156, 166
Healey, Captain Claude AIF, 106
HERMES, HMS, British aircraft
    carrier, sinking, 71
Hintok Camp, Burma Railway, 91
Hiroshima (atomic bomb), 123, 131
Hong Kong, 6
Hunt, Major Bruce AAMC, MBE,
    84, 95, 114, 156, 165–72
Hutchinson, Lieutenant
    Colonel, 169

IDZUMO, HIJNS, Japanese
    Cruiser, 11–12
International Red Cross, 160
Imperial Japanese Army (IJA), 83,
    165–6
Ipoh, Malaya, 89
Itagaki, General, IJA, 110–11, 124

Japanese Naval Landing Party
    (Marines), 9, 13

Java, 56, 63–9
Johore Bahru, Malaya, 111

Kanchanaburi Camp, Burma
 Railway, 87, 90, 106, 155–60,
 165, 172
Kedah, north west Malayan state, 35
Kedah Peak, Malaya, 45–6
Kelian Intan, Malayan town in
 Perak state, 47
Kempeitai, Japanese Military
 Police, 111–13
Kennedy, Captain E.C.,
 RN (captain of HMS
 RAWALPINDI 1939), 33
Keyzar, George and Maisie, 56–7
Kinsayok Camp, Burma Railway,
 88, 91,
Konkoita Camp, Burma Railway,
 92, 148, 156–7
Korea, walking holiday, 1938:
 Count Stefano Macchi di
 Celerre, 26–7
 Diamond Mountains,
 Kumgangsan (Mount
 Kumgang), 24–31
 'One Arm Sutton'
 (Major General Frank
 Sutton, MC), 25
 people, language and
 countryside, 29–30
 travel and Japanese attitudes,
 24–8
Korean guards Burma Railway,
 147–8
Kota Bharu, Malaya, 35

KRAIT, MFV, 109, 113
 see also Operation *Jaywick*
Kuala Lumpur, Malaya, 89
Kuantan, Malayan town on east
 coast, 36

Laird, Henry, brother of Richard
 Laird:
 death in motorcycle accident
 1941, 46–7
 marriage to Barbara Faraday, xi
 Morgan Three Wheelers,
 'Yellow' and 'Red', xii
 work for Michael McEvoy,
 motor engineers, xi–xii
Laird, Marjorie ('Maudie'), sister
 of Richard Laird, xi, 16, 21,
 28, 42, 46
Laird, Mary, mother of Richard
 Laird, xi
Laird, Richard, ('Dick' or 'Dickie'):
 early years and education, xi
 letters to Bobbie following
 release from Changi, 127–33
 motorbikes, Brough Superior
 and Ariel 'Red Hunter', xii,
 47–8, 50
 Prisoner of War, Changi
 1942–1943:
 diet and food, 70, 72–4
 execution of Chinese and
 British POWs, 71, 75
 Red Cross supplies, 76
 'Selarang Incident', 74–6,
 trade with Singapore
 Chinese, 72

Prisoner of War, Burma
   Railway 1943:
   arrival at Songkurai No.2
      Camp, 82, 94–5
   cholera isolation hospital at
      Songkurai No.2 Camp, 98
   elephants at work on Railway,
      100–101
   evacuation to Tanbaya and
      treatment, 101, 103–104
   evacuation from Tanbaya to
      Changi, 105–107
   march from Ban Pong to
      Songkurai No.2 Camp,
      87–94
   radio at Songkurai No.2
      Camp, 98–100
   Railway work at Songkurai
      No.2 Camp, 97
   selection of personnel for 'F'
      Force, 85
   train journey Singapore to
      Ban Pong, 86
Prisoner of War Changi and
   Freedom 1943–1945:
   Changi activities, 116–18
   Changi news service, 118
   food and vegetable gardening
      in Changi, 115–16
   letter 'in event of my death',
      119–20
   life in Changi, 113–14,
   officers' 'pay' in Changi, 116
return to Singapore 1946, 53, 141
rise of Nazis and decision to
   join the TA, 4

Shanghai 1937–1939:
   life in Shanghai, 5–7, 15–16,
      19, 23–4
   playing rugger [sic], 31–2
   Settlement Police, 7
   Sino-Japanese Hostilities
      and service with, xii, 3, 8,
      11–12
   Shanghai Volunteer Corps
      1937, 8–23
Singapore and Penang 1939 to
   1941:
   commissioning into Royal
      Army Service Corps, 39,
      41, 43
   first meeting with
      Bobbie Couper Patrick,
      39–40
   re-union with Bobbie
      December 1941, 52–6
   service on Penang Island,
      war and evacuation, 42,
      44–50
   service with RASC West
      Force, Johore, 54–5
   Singapore Royal Artillery
      (Volunteer) 'The Battery',
      38, 41
   wedding of Sherwood
      Connor and Betty
      Gordon, 39–40
views on Chamberlain and
   appeasement, xii, 28–9
walking holiday in Korea, 1938,
   24–31
   see also Korea

work for Sun Insurance Office, xii, 37–8
Laird, Roy MacGregor ('RML'), xi
Le Mesurier, Guy, 72–3, 114
Lingga Archipelago, Java Sea, 37
Lockheed Lightning fighter, 121
Lyon, Lieutenant Colonel Ivan, MBE, DSO, Gordon Highlanders, 51, 109–10, 113

Madras, 127–8, 130
Malaya POW Administration (Japanese), 147, 159
MARELLA, SS, 67
Melbourne, Australia, xiii, 68, 78–80, 95–6
Michael McEvoy, motor engineers, xi–xii
 see also Laird, Henry
Ministry of Economic Warfare (MEW), 36
Miskin, Mr, Bobbie's SOE boss in Singapore, 55
Mott, Lieutenant Colonel Egerton, SRD Melbourne, 68
Mountbatten, Admiral, SEAC, 110–11
Mudie, James, Royal Corps of Signals, 99

Nagasaki (atomic bomb), 123, 131
Narrative of 'F' Force in Thailand 1943, Report, 145–52
Nippon Slaves, by Lionel de Rosario, 82, 173

Northumberland Fusiliers, 9th Battalion, 102–103, 167

Ogley, Brian, BOAC, 66–7
Operation *Jaywick*, 109–13
Operation *Rimau*, 110–11
Outram Road Jail, 83

Padang Besar, Malaya, 89
Padang, West Sumatra, 51, 62, 153
Palembang, Sumatra, 65, 67
Palmer, Edith, (companion on Korean holiday 1938), 24
PANGKOR, Straits Steamship, evacuation of Penang, 50
Pearl Harbour, Hawaii, American naval base, 35
Penang Island, Malaya:
 Batu Ferringhi Beach, 141
 fall and evacuation, 49–50
 ferries *TANJONG* and *BAGAN*, 49
 Georgetown, 49
 Glugor Cantonment, RASC HQ, 45
 Lone Pine Hotel, 141
Perlis, north west Malayan State, 35
Phillips, Admiral Sir Tom, 36
Pickering, John, Head of Force 136 Malayan Section, 126
Pontian Kecil, Johore, Malaya, 55
PORPOISE, HMS, British submarine, 110
 see also Operation *Rimau*

Pottinger, Pat (Richard Laird's boss in Shanghai), 24
PRINCE OF WALES, HMS, battleship, sinking, 35–6, 50
Prince, Ralph, ('The Loyals') and Leila, 69
Prisoners of War in Thailand 1943, Report on, 153–63

Qing Dynasty, 1

RAJPUTANA, RMS, P&O Liner, 4
Rapide, De Havilland, 38
RAWALPINDI, RMS, P&O Liner and Armed Merchant Cruiser, 33
Recovery of Allied Prisoners of War and Internees (RAPWI), 128, 130–1, 136, 140
Red Cross letters, 25-word, xiii, 63, 70, 78, 85, 112
Red Cross supplies, 76, 86, 125
REPULSE, HMS, battlecruiser, sinking, 35–6, 50
Reynolds, Bill, 109
Riau Archipelago, Java Sea, 37, 109
Rising Sun Petroleum Company, 98
River Kwai Noi, Thailand, 82, 100
Ross, Mai-mai, (companion on Korean holiday 1938), 24, 27–8
Rouchi, Burma, 103

Saito, Lieutenant, IJA, 166
Sandakan Death Marches, Borneo, 138
SCHARNHORST, German battlecruiser, 33
Segamat, town in northern Johore, Malaya, 54
Selarang Incident, Changi, 74–6
Shanghai:
   Cricket Club, 5–9
   International Settlement and French Concession, 1
   Nanking Road, 11, 15, 39
   population 1936, 1
   Race Club and Shanghai Art Museum, 2
   Race Course and Peoples' Square, 2
   Russians, refugees from the Revolution, 7–8
   Settlement Police, 7
Shanghai Volunteer Corps and Shanghai Scottish, 9–23
Shanghai Sino-Japanese Hostilities 1937:
   'Bloody Saturday' bombings, 14 August 1937, 11, 19
   Chinese tactics and withdrawal, 13–14
   evacuation of British dependents, 12, 21
   Japanese shelling and bombing, 9–10, 19–20
   Japanese actions and attitudes, 22–3
   North Station and 'Windy Corner', 9–10
   origins, 8–9

Soochow Creek, 13, 16–17
  see also Laird, Richard
Shimo Nieke Camp, Burma
    Railway, 92, 156–8
Singapore:
  Alexandra Hospital, Japanese
    atrocities, 61
  Balmoral Road, 53
  Barker Road, 52–3
  Bishopsgate, No 1, Bachelor
    Mess, 38, 40, 57
  Bukit Sembawang Estate, 55
  Causeway, 55, 57, 62, 111
  Changi, 69–80, 112–26
  Collyer Quay, 56, 63, 78,
    123, 140
  Ewe Boon Road, 53, 141
  Fort Canning, HQ Singapore
    Fortress, 53, 61
  Naval Base, Sembawang, 44
  Nee Soon, 59
  Outram Road Jail, 83
  Oxley Rise, 53, 56
  Padang, British 25 pdr guns, 62
  River Valley Road Camp, 76
  Sembawang Rubber Estate, 114
  Singapore Harbour Board, 57,
    59–62
  Singapore Volunteer Corps
    (SVC), 38
  Singapore Royal Artillery
    (Volunteer), SRA(V), 38
  Sime Road Civilian Detention
    Camp, 111, 114
  Straits of Johore, 71
  Tanglin Club, 40

Tengah Aerodrome, 112
Thomson Road, 57–9
Singapore's Dunkirk, by Geoffrey
    Brooke, 37, 142, 173
SOE Singapore 1941/42, by
    Richard Gough, 51, 173
Songkurai No.1 Camp, (Shimo
    Songkurai), Burma Railway,
    92, 161
Songkurai No.2 Camp,
    (Naka Songkurai),
    Burma Railway:
  conditions on arrival, 82, 94
  cholera and cholera hospital,
    95, 98–100
  daily death rate, 151
  evacuation of sick men,
    101–102, 166
  radio, 98–100
  Railway work, 97
  selection of men for work, 159
  see also Laird, Richard
Songkurai No.3 Camp, (Kami
    Songkurai), Burma Railway,
    160–1
Special Operations Executive
    (SOE), Far East:
  Force 136, SOE Mission in
    India, 68
  Oriental Mission, Singapore,
    36, 52
  Services Reconaissance
    Department, Australia,
    68, 78
Special Order of the Day, 60
  see also Wavell, General

Spencer Chapman, Lieutenant Colonel Freddie, DSO and Bar, 52
Stewart, Lieutenant Colonel Bob, SOE, 111, 125
Straits Settlement Currency, 73
SUFFOLK, HMS, British cruiser, 15
Sumatra, 51, 62, 153,
Sun Insurance Office Limited, xii, 79, 140
SUSSEX, HMS, British cruiser, 110
Sutton, Major General Frank, MC, 25
Sydney, Australia, 68, 78
Syonan Shimbum, Japanese newspaper, 77–8

Tameron Pa Camp, Burma Railway, 92
Tanara Camp, Burma Railway, 90
Tanbaya 'F' Force Hospital Camp, Burma, 84, 99–105, 160
Tanbaya Hospital, Burma, Medical Report 1943:
 drug shortages, 168
 nutrition and diet, 167–8
 rationale and setting up, 165–6
 staff and administration, 169–70
 tropical diseases and mortality, 168, 170–2
Tarkanoon Camp, Burma Railway, 92
Tarso Camp, Burma Railway, 90

TEGELBERG, MV, Dutch Liner, 40–1
Temple Camp, Burma Railway, 90
Terauchi, Count, Field Marshal, IJA, 110, 124
Thai Labour Corps, 156
Thanbyuzayat, Burma, 81, 103, 129
The Heroes of 'F' Force, by Don Wall, 85, 142, 174
The Hump, 121
The Judy Story, by E. Varley, 58, 174
The Jungle is Neutral, by F. Spencer-Chapman, 52
Three Pagodas Pass, Burma, 81, 87–8, 99, 101–103, 148
Tjilatjap, Java, 67
Tonchang Camp, Burma Railway, 91
Towards the Setting Sun, by James Bradley, 83, 100, 173
Treaty of Nanking 1842, 1
Treaty Ports, 1, 32
Trincomalee, Ceylon, 71
Turner, Lieutenant, Doctor, FMS Volunteer Force, 98–9

Vickers, Dame Joan, 130
Vickers *Wildebeest*, torpedo bomber, 54
Von Duhn, Friedrich, Professor of Archeology, Heidelberg University, xii
Von Duhn, Klara Burger, 3

Wakabayashi, Lieutenant, IJA, 105, 159
Walters, Johnnie, 106
War Crimes Trial, 'F' Force, Burma-Siam Railway, 83, 145
Warren, Colonel Alan George, CBE, DSC, Royal Marines, 36, 50–2, 153
Wavell, General, 59–60
Wearnes Air Services, De Havilland *Rapides*, 38
Whampoa (Huangpu) River, 2, 9, 11–13
Whampoa Road, 15
Wild, Major Cyril H.D.:
   death in air crash Kai Tak, 83
   'F' Force Japanese interpreter, 83, 97–100, 115, 145, 152–3, 156
   War Crimes Liaison Officer, Malaya and Singapore, 83, 111
Wusih, 15

Yangtze Kiang, river, 16, 22
Yamashita, General, IJA, 98, 162